At Issue

| Wind Farms

Other Books in the At Issue Series:

At Issue

Wind Farms

Amy Francis, Book Editor

GREENHAVEN PRESS
A part of Gale, Cengage Learning

GALE
CENGAGE Learning·

Farmington Hills, Mich • San Francisco • New York • Waterville, Maine
Meriden, Conn • Mason, Ohio • Chicago

Patricia Coryell, *Vice President & Publisher, New Products & GVRL*
Douglas Dentino, *Manager, New Products*
Judy Galens, *Acquisitions Editor*

For more information, contact:
Greenhaven Press
27500 Drake Rd.
Farmington Hills, MI 48331-3535
Or you can visit our Internet site at gale.cengage.com

For product information and technology assistance, contact us at

Gale Customer Support, 1-800-877-4253
For permission to use material from this text or product, submit all requests online at www.cengage.com/permissions

Further permissions questions can be e-mailed to permissionrequest@cengage.com

Articles in Greenhaven Press anthologies are often edited for length to meet page requirements. In addition, original titles of these works are changed to clearly present the main thesis and to explicitly indicate the author's opinion. Every effort is made to ensure that Greenhaven Press accurately reflects the original intent of the authors. Every effort has been made to trace the owners of copyrighted material.

Cover image © Debra Hughes 2007. Used under license from Shutterstock.com.

LIBRARY OF CONGRESS CATALOGING-IN-PUBLICATION DATA

Wind farms / Amy Francis, book editor.
    pages cm. -- (At issue)
    Includes bibliographical references and index.
    ISBN 978-0-7377-7203-6 (hardcover) -- ISBN 978-0-7377-7204-3 (pbk.)
    1. Wind power plants--Juvenile literature. 2. Wind power plants--Environmental aspects--Juvenile literature. 3. Wind power plants--Government policy--Juvenile literature. I. Francis, Amy.
    TK1541.W5555 2015
    333.9'2--dc23
                             2014030228

Printed in Mexico
1 2 3 4 5 6 7 19 18 17 16 15

Contents

Introduction

Wind farms dot the landscape in thirty-nine of the fifty states across America, accounting for over forty-six thousand turbines countrywide. Worldwide, wind turbines can be found in seventy-nine countries. As they spread in popularity across the globe, it's not difficult to find a wide range of opinion in the scientific community about their value, making for considerable debate whenever a new wind project proposal is placed before a community. While the science may still be emerging, what people know for certain is how they feel when they see a group of spinning turbines. While some find them beautiful, others think they destroy the beauty of existing landscapes and skylines. The visual impact of a proposed turbine is often the most contentious and publicized issue of public objection.

As community residents debate the pros and cons of wind turbines on a local level, government and other officials often express their opinions in the news. Joe Hockey, the treasurer of Australia, describes wind turbines as "utterly offensive." As quoted on a radio talk show, he adds, "I think they're a blight on the landscape."[1] Dame Helen Ghosh, director general of the National Trust, an organization tasked with preserving historic places and landscapes in the United Kingdom, states, "Personally, I think a wind turbine in the right place is a rather beautiful thing. I think they can look graceful . . . and because of the importance of renewable energy—we don't object to them."[2] She continues to say she believes someday they will be viewed in the same light that railways are viewed now.

1. Quoted in Oliver Milman, "Joe Hockey Tilts at Wind Turbines," *The Guardian*, May 1, 2014. http://www.theguardian.com/world/2014/may/02/wind-turbines-are-utterly -offensive-joe-hockey-tells-alan-jones.
2. Quoted in Ben Bryant, "National Trust Director-General: Wind Turbines Are 'Beautiful,'" *The Telegraph*, February 24, 2013. http://www.telegraph.co.uk/earth /energy/windpower/9890649/National-Trust-director-general-Wind-turbines-are -beautiful.html.

Others do not see such a bright future for the turbines and believe no matter how one feels about them now, the turbines will become blight. According to Jay Lehr, writing in *Heartlander Magazine*:

> Few of these turbines will last 20 years ... [and few] companies have the financial reserves to dismantle these behemoth lawn sculptures. Just as it has taken massive subsidies to build the vast industrial wind installations, it will likely take massive subsidies to dismantle them. The resulting scene of permanent wind sculptures, monuments to the triumph of political favoritism over science and economics, will be frozen in time like a scene from science fiction.[3]

The visual impact of wind turbines, however, has not escaped the scientific community entirely, and there may be a way to measure the visual impact on a community—in home values. Whether they are viewing them out the car window on a road trip or out a kitchen window may make a big difference in how people feel about wind farms. Numerous studies have explored home values in the areas surrounding new wind farm developments without finding a significant relationship between the two. For example, in a blog for the Union of Concerned Scientists, John Rogers, a senior energy analyst, reported on a study that looked at home values in Massachusetts and "found no evidence that home values are affected by proximity to wind turbines."[4] Other studies conducted by the University of New Hampshire, the Centre for Economics and Business Research, the University of Rhode Island, and many other organizations had similar findings.

The most recent study, however, by Stephen Gibbons with the Spatial Economics Research Centre at the London School

---

3. Jay Lehr, "Wind Turbines: American's Vast, Ugly Sculpture Garden," *Heartlander Magazine*, July 16, 2013. http://news.heartland.org/newspaper-article/2013/07/16/wind-turbines-americas-vast-ugly-sculpture-garden.
4. John Rogers, "The Effect of Wind Turbines on Property Values: A New Study in Massachusetts Provides Some Answers," Union of Concerned Scientists, January 22, 2014. http://blog.ucsusa.org/effect-of-wind-turbines-on-property-values-384.

of Economics and Political Science, reported that "operational wind farm developments reduce prices in locations where the turbines are visible, relative to where they are not visible, and that the effects are causal."[5]

Like the wind itself, opinions can change. Following a proposal for twelve turbines above Ardrossan, a small seaside town on the west coast of Scotland, there was considerable community objection. After a year, however, one of the town's councilors wrote: "The Ardrossan wind farm has been overwhelmingly accepted by local people—instead of spoiling the landscape, we believe it has been enhanced. The turbines are impressive looking, bring a calming effect to the town and, contrary to the belief that they would be noisy, we have found them to be silent workhorses."[6]

It may be that those who oppose wind farms based on their appearance are focused on the wrong thing. In an anonymous editorial in *The Independent*, the author points out that over two-thirds of wind farm plans failed in mainland Britain because local councils rejected them. The author states, "No one is suggesting that developers are given carte blanche to erect turbines across areas of outstanding natural beauty. . . . That wind turbines are ugly has become an accepted truth of the onshore wind debate. . . . But should a judgment so subjective be allowed to drive policy on something so important as energy policy?"[7]

The authors of the viewpoints in *At Issue: Wind Farms* address the importance of wind energy to the environment and

5. Stephen Gibbons, "Gone with the Wind: Valuing the Visual Impacts of Wind Turbines through House Prices," Spatial Economics Research Center, April 2014. http://www.spatialeconomics.ac.uk/textonly/SERC/publications/download/sercdp0159.pdf.

6. Quoted in Simon Gourlay, "Wind Farms Are Not Only Beautiful, They're Absolutely Necessary," *The Guardian*, August 11, 2008. http://www.theguardian.com/commentisfree/2008/aug/12/windpower.alternativeenergy.

7. "The Conservatives Are Deciding Wind Farm Applications on the Basis of Their Appearance. This is Misguided," *Independent*, June 11, 2014. http://www.independent.co.uk/voices/editorials/the-conservatives-are-deciding-wind-farm-applications-on-the-basis-of-their-appearance-this-is-misguided-9522980.html.

world economy and highlight both the benefits and drawbacks of the technologies currently used to harness the wind as a source of clean and renewable energy.

1

America Should Continue to Invest in Wind Energy

Jordan Schneider, Tony Dutzik, and Rob Sargent

Jordan Schneider is an analyst and Tony Dutzik a senior policy analyst for the Frontier Group. Rob Sargent is the energy program director for Environment America.

Tax credits that encourage construction of new wind turbines are key to the success of wind energy. Although the initial costs of wind energy are expensive, the investment will result in reliable, sustainable energy and additional jobs in the United States. In addition to continuing wind energy tax credits, the US government must establish renewable electricity standards to ensure market demand for wind energy will continue. Finally, the United States should make use of offshore wind to maximize wind energy's potential.

America's clean energy boom is no accident. It is the direct result of strong, forward-thinking policies adopted over the last decade at both the state and federal levels, policies that have unleashed the energy of innovative companies and American workers to fuel dramatic growth in renewable energy. As wind energy and other forms of clean, renewable energy take root in the United States—delivering ample benefits for our environment and economy—now is not the time to turn our back on further progress. To further reduce global warming pollution, curb smog and soot, move away from fossil fuels, save water, and grow our economy, the United States should make a long-term commitment to renewable energy with policies to support growth of the wind industry.

Federal Tax Incentives Are Key

Two of the most important tools that have helped grow the wind industry in the United States are the federal renewable electricity production tax credit (PTC) and the investment tax credit (ITC).

Policies such as the PTC and ITC recognize that renewable energy is a key component of an electricity grid that is not only cleaner but that also delivers stable, reasonable prices for consumers. Renewable energy sources such as wind are not subject to the fuel price volatility of coal and natural gas, and can deliver reliable, affordable electricity for decades, making them a smart long-term investment in the nation's energy future. However, renewable energy projects are often capital intensive. Unlike fossil fuel power plants, for which fuel costs represent a significant share of the overall cost of producing power, the vast majority of the costs of building a wind turbine or installing a solar panel are incurred before the first kilowatt-hour of electricity is produced. Public policies that defray some of those initial capital costs, or that help assure a reliable rate of return over the long term, can reduce the risk for investors—opening the floodgates for investment and the rapid expansion of renewable energy.

Federal renewable energy tax credits have been a key contributor to the growth of wind energy over the last decade.

The PTC provides an income tax credit of 2.3 cents per kilowatt-hour (kWh) for utility-scale wind energy producers. It is available for electricity generated during the first 10 years of the wind farm's operation. After expiring at the end of 2012, the PTC was renewed in January 2013 and will be available for all projects that begin construction on or before December 31, 2013.

The investment tax credit (ITC) covers up to 30 percent of the capital cost of new renewable energy investments, with the credit becoming available the moment the wind energy system is placed into service. The ITC also expires on December 31, 2013.

Wind energy developers and other builders of renewable energy systems may choose to take advantage of either the PTC or the ITC, but not both. Different types of renewable energy projects stand to reap greater benefits from one or the other program, depending in part on the capital intensity of the project and the amount of power it produces over time. Federal renewable energy tax credits have been a key contributor to the growth of wind energy over the last decade, but their effectiveness has been hamstrung by their "here today, gone tomorrow" inconsistency. Over the past 13 years, the renewable energy PTC has been available only sporadically. When the PTC has been renewed by Congress for only for one or two years at a time or even allowed to expire, the ensuing uncertainty has discouraged wind developers from building new capacity, stunting industry growth. For instance, in 2000, 2002 and 2004—years when the PTC was allowed to expire temporarily—new wind installations dropped by 93 percent, 73 percent and 77 percent, respectively, from the previous year when the PTC had been in force.

The economic uncertainty created by the sporadic availability of incentives discourages businesses that manufacture turbines, gear boxes, blades, bearings and towers from entering the market or expanding, restricting the supply chain and increasing costs. On the other hand, long-term consistency in renewable energy policy can encourage new businesses to enter the field and expand operations, bringing new jobs and investment to the United States. For example, between 2005–2006 and 2012—a period of relative stability in clean energy incentives—the amount of domestically produced content in U.S. wind power projects increased from 25 percent to 72 percent, creating new jobs and economic opportunity in the United States.

Establish Renewable Electricity Standards and Offshore Wind Resources

A renewable electricity standard (RES) helps support wind energy development by requiring utilities to obtain a percentage of the electricity they provide to consumers from renewable sources. These standards help ensure that wind energy producers have a market for the electricity they generate, as electricity suppliers seek to reach their required threshold for renewable electricity. This certainty makes it easier for wind developers to finance and build new wind power installations. Today, 29 states have renewable electricity standards. From 1999 through 2012, 69 percent of all new wind capacity was built in states with renewable electricity standards. In 2012, the proportion rose to 83 percent. Some of the states with the strongest standards, such as Colorado, have seen the greatest growth in wind power generation.

> *Some of the best wind energy resources are offshore. To capture that potential, policymakers need to set a bold goal for offshore wind development in the Atlantic.*

Renewable electricity standards have not only proven to be effective at spurring wind energy development, but they have also had little effect on ratepayers, with most policies resulting in either a small net benefit or a small cost to ratepayers on the order of $5 per year. This does not include the economic value of the environmental and public health benefits of renewable energy, nor does it reflect the economic benefits of wind energy-driven job creation, leading to the conclusion that renewable electricity standards are a winner for both the environment and the economy.

In order for RES policies to continue to drive wind energy growth, however, states without RESs will need to adopt them, those with policies will need to strengthen them, and the federal government will need to adopt a national policy of its own. According to the U.S. Department of Energy, existing state RESs will drive the addition of only 3 to 5 GW of renewable energy per year between now and the end of the decade, which is lower than the amount of wind energy added in recent years. Strengthening the nation's renewable energy goals will help keep the United States on pace to tap an increasing share of its wind energy potential.

Some of the best wind energy resources are offshore. To capture that potential, policymakers need to set a bold goal for offshore wind development in the Atlantic. A goal will help articulate the important role of offshore wind in America's energy future. The Department of the Interior and the Bureau of Ocean Energy Management will need sufficient staff and resources to manage multiple renewable energy leases along the coast and to promote an efficient leasing process. A coordinated effort by federal, state and regional economic development, energy and commerce agencies is needed to develop commitments to purchase offshore wind power. Finally, offshore wind projects must be sited, constructed and operated responsibly in order to avoid and mitigate conflict with local marine life and other uses.

2

Wind Farms Should Not Receive Government Funding

Mike Bond

Mike Bond is an environmental activist and renewable energy advocate.

Wind energy is a terrible idea, particularly for a state like Maine. Studies show that wind energy neither reduces fossil fuel use nor lowers greenhouse gas emissions. The money spent on wind projects would be better invested in other alternative, more environmentally friendly sources of fuel. For this reason, the government should stop subsidies for wind energy projects.

As a lifelong Democrat, environmental activist and renewable energy advocate, I commend Gov. [Paul] LePage's recent criticisms of the huge taxpayer-funded industrial wind power scam, which, unless it is stopped, will ruin Maine.

Though initially a proponent of industrial wind, I've learned it's a catastrophe on every level—environmental, fiscal, social and economic.

And now with Maine's southern neighbors halting industrial wind in their states, they're paying to build thousands of turbines in Maine, to devastate every magnificent Maine ridge, pinnacle and mountain with howling machines more than 50 stories high, some so tall they'll be the third-tallest structures in New England.

Industrial wind projects have been clearly proven to slaughter millions of birds and bats, destroy scenic beauty, lower property values and tourism, sicken people and drive them from their homes, increase erosion and raise electric rates. But they make billions in taxpayer-funded subsidies for the investment banks that develop them.

Wind Doesn't Reduce the Need for Fossil Fuels

Yet the biggest trouble with industrial wind is it doesn't lower greenhouse gas emissions or fossil fuel use. Not one molecule. The reason is that winds (particularly in Maine) are erratic, and as a result, industrial wind "farms" have to be backed up constantly by "fixed" generation, e.g., fossil fuel plants. This problem, called "spinning reserve," basically invalidates any claim that wind projects lower fossil fuel use or CO_2 generation.

Online, one can find numerous scientific, utility and environmental studies showing that despite nearly three decades of huge federal subsidies, industrial wind projects don't lower greenhouse gas emissions or fossil fuel use, and in some cases, they even increase them. In Germany and Britain, for instance, development of wind projects has led to an escalation in coal use.

Even industrial wind developers admit the capacity of wind projects in Maine is only 25 percent of their advertised amount.

This is without even considering the extensive greenhouse gases produced by constructing these huge towers; shipping them across the ocean; trucking them to wherever the wind industry has overridden the local folks and imposed a wind "farm," and building them.

Consider a typical Maine wind "farm" advertised as 100 megawatts, about 35 turbine towers.

Because Maine winds are poor, turbines run at a low rate, sometimes as little as four days a month. Even industrial wind developers admit the capacity of wind projects in Maine is only 25 percent of their advertised amount. Thus, a 100-megawatt project only creates 25 megawatts.

But even when the turbines are turning, the power can't always be used, such as at night, so utilities curtail or "dump" it. In Maine, this reduces our wind project's used power to barely 17 megawatts. And because most wind electricity will be transmitted out of Maine to Connecticut or Massachusetts, the transmission loss could exceed 5 percent, lowering this to 16.6 megawatts.

But one also has to deduct the fuel to run the spinning reserve, which means the real power provided to electricity consumers by a 100-megawatt industrial wind project is barely 8 percent of advertised capacity—8 megawatts, not 100 megawatts.

This 8 megawatts is disastrously low for a project that could cost taxpayers $300 million. By comparison, an 8-megawatt gas-fired power plant could be built for under $15 million and would create far less CO_2. Or, for the same $300 million, we could equip 20,000 Maine homes and businesses with rooftop solar, and significantly reduce Maine's CO_2 emissions.

Ever noticed the turbines turning when there's no wind? To keep them from seizing up, they have to be turned by buying electricity. This is why three of the largest electricity consumers in Maine are wind projects—they each use more power than Maine's largest pulp mill.

I may not agree with Gov. LePage on everything, but he has clearly enunciated an absolute truth for Maine. If we care about the beauty of our precious state, the superb individuality of our Maine people and the enormous economic engine that this beauty and cohesion represents, then we must all, Democrats, independents and Republicans, stand for what is right for Maine and reject what is wrong.

We hear a lot of pro-wind commercials on the Maine Public Broadcasting Network, and a lot of pro-wind talk from groups like Maine Audubon, the Sierra Club of Maine and the Natural Resources Council of Maine. Guess why? Many such organizations get major funding from industrial wind developers.

Years ago I learned a lot about life as a *Portland Press Herald* paper boy, delivering it sometimes in a blizzard at 30 below, but I made sure my customers got their papers. That's a spirit Maine inculcates: fairness and reliability. Industrial wind projects have neither.

3

The Government Should End Wind Subsidies and Encourage Innovation

Geoffrey Styles

Geoffrey Styles is managing director of GSW Strategy Group, LLC, an energy and environmental strategy consulting firm.

The continued US tax credits for wind energy do nothing to encourage the development of innovative technologies that could make renewable energy more affordable in the future. Energy tax credits for other renewable energies decreased as the technology advanced, which is a much better model in the long run. Although tax credits were good for getting companies started in wind energy, continued government investment in wind does nothing to further the technology.

With the end of the year fast approaching, the US wind power industry faces yet another scheduled expiration of federal tax credits for new wind turbines. The wind Production Tax Credit, or PTC, was due to expire at the end of 2012 but was extended for an additional year as part of last December's [2012] "fiscal cliff" deal. There are no signs yet of a similar reprieve this year. [The credit expired at the end of 2013.]

With the PTC and other energy-related "tax expenditures" subject to Congressional negotiations on tax reform, this might truly be its last hurrah in its current form. It is high time for this overly generous subsidy to be "sunsetted," and if it's replaced with a smarter policy emphasizing innovation, the outcome could be beneficial for taxpayers, the environment, and even the US wind energy industry.

The Tax Credit Is Too Big

In its 20-year history, minus a few year-long expirations in the past, the PTC has promoted tremendous growth in the US wind industry, from under 2,000 MW [megawatts] of installed wind capacity in 1992 to over 60,000 MW as of today. For most of its tenure, the PTC did exactly what it was intended to do: reward developers for generating increasing amounts of renewable electricity for the grid at a rate tied to inflation.

Before reflexively supporting or opposing another PTC [Production Tax Credit] extension, depending on one's politics, we should ask what we'd be getting for that $5 or $6 billion.

However, unlike the federal investment tax credit for solar power and some other renewables, the amount of the subsidy didn't automatically decrease as wind power technology improved, with wind turbines growing steadily larger, more efficient, and cheaper to build. Instead, the PTC's subsidy for wind power increased from 1.5 ¢ per kilowatt-hour (kWh) to its present level of around 2.3 ¢. That's roughly one-third of today's average US retail electricity price for industrial customers and exceeds most estimates of typical operating and maintenance costs for wind power. The latter point has serious implications for the impact of wind farms on other generators in a regional power grid.

If wind turbine installations continued at their remarkably depressed rate of just 64 MW in the first three quarters of this year, the cost of extending the PTC for another year would be negligible. However, it's evident from industry data that a major reason installations are so low in 2013 is that the uncertainty over last year's scheduled expiration caused developers to accelerate projects into the record-setting fourth quarter of 2012. The American Wind Energy Association cites over 2,300 MW of new wind capacity under construction as of the end of September, while installations over the last three years averaged just under 8,400 MW annually.

At that rate, a one-year extension of the current PTC would add around $5 billion to the federal budget over the 10 years that new wind farms would receive benefits. Congress's Joint Committee on Taxation apparently came up with a slightly higher estimate of $6.1 billion.

High Wind Subsidies Offer Less Bang for the Buck

Before reflexively supporting or opposing another PTC extension, depending on one's politics, we should ask what we'd be getting for that $5 or $6 billion. One of the commonest rationales I encounter justifying the continuation of the PTC is that conventional energy continues to receive billions of dollars in subsidies each year. Without getting bogged down in arguments over the definition of a subsidy, or the real and imagined externalities associated with using fossil fuels, it is certainly true that the US oil and gas industry benefits from deductions and tax credits in the federal tax code to the tune of around $4.3 billion per year, based on figures in the latest White House budget.

If we compare these benefits on the basis of the energy production they yield, the PTC starts to look pretty expensive. For example, wind capacity additions in 2012 of over 13,100 MW increased wind generation by 20 billion kWh over the previous year. That's the energy equivalent of about 140 billion cubic feet of natural gas in power generation, or 66,000 barrels per day of oil. (Although less than 1% of US oil consumption is used to generate electricity, oil is still an easily visualized common denominator.)

By comparison, US oil production expanded by 837,000 bbl/day, while natural gas production grew by the equivalent of another 606,000 bbl/day. So on this somewhat apples-to-oranges basis, oil and gas added more than 20 times as much new energy output to the US economy as wind power did, for roughly the same cost to the federal government.

Now, it's true that domestic oil and gas both had banner years in 2012, in terms of growth, reversing longer-term decline trends in earlier years, but US wind had its biggest year ever last year. Another factor making this comparison more reasonable than it might otherwise seem is that these are all essentially mature technologies. Wind turbines are still improving, but these improvements are mainly incremental at this point. Nor do they or the billions in annual subsidies for wind address the single biggest obstacle to the wider adoption of wind energy, arising from its fundamental intermittency and disjunction with typical daily and seasonal electricity demand cycles.

Now is the ideal time to reconsider the thinking behind the Production Tax Credit.

Time to Refocus on Innovation

When the PTC was first implemented in 1992, by its very existence it fostered innovation in a technology that was still in its infancy as a commercial means of generating meaningful quantities of electricity. That's no longer the case. I've seen various ideas for reforming the PTC to make it more innovation-focused, but while these might be preferable to the status quo, they strike me as overly narrow. We don't just need wind innovation, but *energy* innovation, and in fact innovation across the whole US economy if we want to remain globally competitive, and if we want to make more than incremental reductions in our greenhouse gas emissions.

It's ironic in that context that the federal 20% research and development [R&D] tax credit is also due to expire at the end of the year. If it came down to a choice between extending the R&D tax credit and extending the PTC, I'd hope that even the wind industry would opt for the R&D credit. That's not entirely a false choice, considering the scale of ongoing federal deficits and debt, and the need for the government to borrow around 20% of what it spends.

Now is the ideal time to reconsider the thinking behind the Production Tax Credit. That's not just because the Congress must shortly decide whether or not to extend it, but because its expiration now wouldn't be as abrupt as was foreseen at the end of 2011 or 2012. Last year's extension redefined how projects qualify for the PTC, so any wind project that has either started significant work or spent 5% of its budget by year-end could still qualify for the current PTC in 2014. I have seen analysis suggesting a project begun now might even qualify after 2015, as long as work on it had been continuous.

This smoother transition gives both Congress and the wind industry time to reevaluate what role, if any, specific wind-energy subsidies have in a national energy economy that looks very different than the one in which the PTC was first conceived in the 1990s, or even when the larger renewable energy incentives of the federal stimulus were adopted in 2009. I'd be very surprised if the outcome of such a deliberation was to simply continue the same two-decade old structure into the future.

4

Wind Energy Cuts Carbon Emissions

Chris Goodall and Mark Lynas

Chris Goodall is a businessman, author, and climate-change expert. Mark Lynas is an author working full time on climate change.

Despite myths to the contrary, wind power does reduce carbon emissions significantly. Opponents of wind energy often focus on the fact that wind power needs to be backed up by more traditional power sources. However, recent data shows that as wind energy becomes more available, coal plants are used less and less. Also, as new technologies emerge, additional means of storing electricity will reduce reliance on back-up sources.

The assertion that wind turbines don't reduce carbon emissions is a myth, according to conclusive statistical data obtained from National Grid and analysed here in the *Guardian* for the first time. With a new wind generation record of 4,131 megawatts set on 14 September [2012], the question of how far the UK's wind generation fleet can help in meeting our climate targets is increasingly controversial. Now it can be shown that the sceptics who lobby against wind simply have their facts wrong.

Wind Back-ups

On 14 September [2012], wind turbines connected to the National Grid produced over 80 gigawatt-hours (GWh) of electricity, just over 10% of total UK generation. This was far from being a one-off: with more than 4,000 turbines both on and offshore now connected to the grid, wind produced 48 GWh of usable electricity per day on average during September, adding up to about 6% of overall daily national electricity requirement. On many days, wind is now the fourth-largest source of UK electricity, after coal, nuclear and gas. Indeed, this figure is a significant underestimate, because about two gigawatts of wind are connected directly to local networks and so not directly visible to National Grid.

However, according to increasingly vocal critics of wind power, the intermittent nature of wind generation means we must burn more gas to provide backup. According to *Telegraph* columnist Christopher Booker:

> Ramping the back-up gas plants up and down would mean running them very inefficiently, and give off so much CO_2 that we could end up increasing our overall emissions rather than reducing them.

Journalist and author Matt Ridley asserts that:

> The total carbon emissions saved by the great wind rush is probably below 1%, because of the need to keep fossil fuels burning as back-up when the wind does not blow. It may even be a negative number.

From analysing National Grid data of more than 4,000 half-hour periods over the last three months, a strong correlation between windiness and a reduction in gas-fired generation becomes clear.

The climate-sceptic Global Warming Policy Foundation (GWPF) recently gave evidence to the House of Commons energy and climate change committee, stating:

> There is a significant risk that annual CO_2 emissions could be greater under the wind scenario than under the gas scenario.

The essence of the wind sceptics' case is that a scaling up in wind power will have to be "backed up" by massive investment in gas-fired open cycle turbine (OCGT) plants, which are cheap to build but considerably less efficient than the combined cycle gas turbine (CCGT) power plants which deliver the vast majority of the UK's gas-fired electricity supply.

Their arguments are not borne out by current statistics, however. If the sceptics were right, the recent windy conditions would have seen considerable use of less-efficient OCGT as wind input to the grid ramped up and down. In actual fact, during the entire June–September period, OCGTs and equally dirty oil-fired stations produced less than one hundredth of one percent of all UK electricity. In total they operated for a grand total of just nine half hour periods in the first 19 days of the month—and these periods had nothing to do with changing windspeeds.

Wind Reduces CO_2

From analysing National Grid data of more than 4,000 half-hour periods over the last three months, a strong correlation between windiness and a reduction in gas-fired generation becomes clear. The exchange rate is about one for one: a megawatt hour of wind typically meant the UK grid used one less megawatt hour of gas-derived electricity. This means that actual CO_2 savings can be calculated from the data with a high degree of accuracy—these are not guesstimates from models, but observations of real-world data.

Over a year, based on the amount of electricity wind is currently generating each day, wind turbines save around 6.1m tonnes of carbon dioxide, or about 4% of the UK's emissions from electricity (based on CCGT plants emitting around 350 kg CO_2 per mWh). This figure provides independent confirmation for the trade body RenewableUK's estimate of a current reduction in annual emissions from the entire UK wind fleet of about 6m tonnes.

Looking to the future, about 26 gigawatts of onshore and offshore wind is expected to be connected to the grid by 2020, nearly four times today's capacity. Even so, National Grid expects to be able to handle the increased wind generation without major new investment in dirty open-cycle gas backup, contradicting the claims from the GWPF.

The National Grid's Gillian West says:

> As more wind connects, there will be a need for additional back-up for that intermittency ... [however] there will be more interconnection with mainland Europe and new storage technologies may also emerge (e.g. battery) or additional pumped storage hydro which can provide short term response.

National Grid is also improving its wind forecasting system to make coping with times of low demand and high generation easier.

When the wind is blowing the UK emits less CO_2 per unit of electricity generated.

Indeed, the wind sceptics may have their case backwards. The biggest blackout risk is not intermittent wind but the threat of total loss of a single giant power source, such as a large coal or nuclear plant, possibly within just a few seconds. But the grid is already engineered to withstand this catastrophic loss with existing back-up—and wind is unlikely to change this picture for the foreseeable future.

The intermittency of wind is balanced both by the inertia of the turbines themselves and by multiple wind installations over a wide geographical area. In addition, wind is now forecasted with reasonable accuracy at least a day in advance, allowing National Grid to plan the right generation mix to accompany it. Indeed, the most difficult issues for the Grid come from the demand side—commercial breaks in Downton

Abbey can lead to sudden demand spikes of hundreds of megawatts in just a few seconds. Wind, in contrast, fades up and down much more slowly.

The researcher Damon Hart-Davis, who maintains a real-time website showing the grid's carbon intensity called Earth Notes, confirms separately that when the wind is blowing the UK emits less CO_2 per unit of electricity generated. This is much more visible currently than it has been in previous years because wind is now a significant enough player to stand out from the statistical noise, which include electricity produced by Welsh pumped-storage hydroelectricity and imports and exports from France, Holland and Ireland.

The UK may be the windiest country in Europe, but other nations already have much greater installed capacity. Spain, for example, occasionally produces 50% of its power from wind turbines with no impact on its electricity grid.

Continued fast expansion in offshore and onshore wind is good news for carbon emissions and can be accommodated without major problems by the grid. Data, not assertions, are what must win the argument over wind—and the data is very clear.

5

Wind Farms Will Create More Carbon Dioxide, Say Scientists

Andrew Gilligan

Andrew Gilligan is a British journalist and editor for the Sunday edition of The Telegraph.

Because of its ability to absorb carbon, peat, which is common in the United Kingdom, is as essential to reducing greenhouse gases from the atmosphere as the rainforest. Wind developers favor inexpensive peatlands when looking for wind farm sites, but many environmentalists are concerned about disturbing the lands and releasing carbon into the atmosphere. Further, extensive road networks built for maintenance around the wind farms aggravate the problem by blocking the flow of water and drying out large areas of peatland. When wind farms are built on peat, so much carbon is released into the atmosphere that some scientists believe the environmental benefits of using wind energy are lost.

Thousands of Britain's wind turbines will create more greenhouse gases than they save, according to potentially devastating scientific research to be published later this year.

The finding, which threatens the entire rationale of the onshore wind farm industry, will be made by Scottish government-funded researchers who devised the standard method used by developers to calculate "carbon payback time" for wind farms on peat soils.

Wind farms are typically built on upland sites, where peat soil is common. In Scotland alone, two thirds of all planned onshore wind development is on peatland. England and Wales also have large numbers of current or proposed peatland wind farms.

But peat is also a massive store of carbon, described as Europe's equivalent of the tropical rainforest. Peat bogs contain and absorb carbon in the same way as trees and plants—but in much higher quantities.

British peatland stores at least 3.2 billion tons of carbon, making it by far the country's most important carbon sink and among the most important in the world.

Wind farms, and the miles of new roads and tracks needed to service them, damage or destroy the peat and cause significant loss of carbon to the atmosphere, where it contributes to climate change.

Writing in the scientific journal *Nature*, the scientists, Dr Jo Smith, Dr Dali Nayak and Prof Pete Smith, of Aberdeen University, say: "We contend that wind farms on peatlands will probably not reduce emissions . . . we suggest that the construction of wind farms on non-degraded peats should always be avoided."

Dr Nayak told *The Telegraph*: "Our full paper is not yet published, but we should definitely be worried about this. If the peatland is already degraded, there is no problem. But if it is in good condition, we should avoid it."

One typical large peat site just approved in southern Scotland, the Kilgallioch wind farm, includes 43 miles of roads and tracks.

Another peat scientist, Richard Lindsay of the University of East London, said: "If we are concerned about CO_2, we shouldn't be worrying first about the rainforests, we should be worrying about peatlands.

"The world's peatlands have four times the amount of carbon than all the world's rainforests. But they are a Cinderella habitat, completely invisible to decision-makers."

One typical large peat site just approved in southern Scotland, the Kilgallioch wind farm, includes 43 miles of roads and tracks. Peat only retains its carbon if it is moist, but the roads and tracks block the passage of the water.

The wind industry insists that it increasingly builds "floating roads," where rock is piled on a textile surface without disturbing the peat underneath.

But Mr Lindsay said: "Peat has less solids in it than milk. The roads inevitably sink, that then causes huge areas of peatland to dry out and the carbon is released."

Mr Lindsay said that more than half of all British onshore wind development, current and planned, is on peat soils.

In 2011 the Scottish government's nature protection body, Scottish Natural Heritage, said 67 per cent of planned onshore wind development in Scotland would be on peatland.

Struan Stevenson, the Tory MEP for Scotland who has campaigned on the issue, said: "This is a devastating blow for the wind factory industry from which I hope it will not recover.

"The Scottish government cannot realise their plans for wind farms without allowing the ruination of peat bogs, so they are trying to brush this problem under the carpet.

"This is just another way in which wind power is a scam. It couldn't exist without subsidy. It is driving industry out of Britain and driving people into fuel poverty."

Scotland's SNP government has led a strong charge for wind power, promising that 100 per cent of the country's electricity will be generated from renewable sources.

But even its environment minister, Stewart Stevenson, admits: "Scotland has 15 per cent of the world's blanket bog.

"Even a small proportion of the carbon stored in peat-lands, if lost by erosion and drainage, could add significantly to our greenhouse gas emissions."

In 2008 Dr Smith, Dr Nayak and Prof Smith devised the standard "carbon payback time" calculator used by the wind farm industry to assess the CO_2 impact of developments on peat soils.

The carbon cost of a badly sited peat wind farm ... was so high that it would take 23 years before it provided any CO_2 benefit.

"Large peatland wind farms introduce high potential for their expected CO_2 savings to be cancelled out by release of greenhouse gases stored in the peat," they said.

"Emission savings are achieved by wind power only after the carbon payback time has elapsed, and if this exceeds the lifetime of the wind farm, no carbon benefits will be realised."

Even the initial version of the calculator found that the carbon cost of a badly sited peat wind farm—on a sloping site, resulting in more drainage of the peat, and without resto-ration afterwards—was so high that it would take 23 years be-fore it provided any CO_2 benefit. The typical life of a wind farm is only 25 years.

The researchers initially believed that well-managed and well-sited peatland wind farms could still cut greenhouse gas emissions, over time, compared to electricity generation over-all.

But now they say that the shrinking use of fossil fuels in overall electricity generation has changed the equation, mak-ing the comparison less favourable to all peatland wind farms.

"Our previous work argued that most peatland sites could save on net [CO_2] emissions," they said. "But emissions factors [in UK electricity generation as a whole] are likely to drop significantly in the future.

"As a result, peatland sites would be less likely to generate a reduction in carbon emissions, even with careful management."

The significance of the Aberdeen researchers' work is increased by the fact that they are funded by the Scottish government and are broadly pro-wind.

They wrote in a previous paper that "it is important that wind farm developments should not be discouraged unnecessarily because they are a key requirement for delivery of the Scottish government's commitment to reduce greenhouse gas emissions."

Helen McDade, from the John Muir Trust, which campaigns to protect wild land, said: "Much of the cheap land being targeted by developers desperate to cash in on wind farm subsidies is peatland in remote wild land areas of the UK.

"This statement, from the academic team who developed the carbon calculator for the Scottish government, is a timely reminder that we must have independent and scientific assessment of the effects of policy and subsidies."

The wind industry insisted that the impact of properly managed wind farms on peat and carbon emissions was minimal. Niall Stuart, director of Scottish Renewables, a trade association, said that damaged peatland could be restored in as little as a year.

He said the association had signed a "statement of good practice principles" with environmental groups promising that "every reasonable effort" will be made to avoid "significant adverse environmental effects" on peatland, including "properly planned and managed habitat restoration."

Jennifer Webber, a spokesman for RenewableUK, the industry lobbying group, said: "Wind farms continue to be an important tool in decarbonisation and energy independence, with actual measurements showing wind displacing gas from the system. This is why they retain support from environmental organisations."

6

Wind Energy Is Reliable

Mark Shwartz

Mark Shwartz writes about energy technology for the Precourt Institute for Energy at Stanford University.

According to a study conducted by scientists at Stanford University, existing energy storage technologies are capable of storing extra energy for when wind or sunlight are not available. Wind produces more additional energy than sun, making wind energy more reliable than solar power. Wind energy is also more cost-effective than solar power because of the extra energy used upfront to produce solar panels. Within the first few months of being installed, wind turbines are able to generate enough energy to replace what was required to create them. As such, wind farms are an excellent source of reliable, sustainable energy.

The worldwide demand for solar and wind power continues to skyrocket. Since 2009, global solar photovoltaic installations have increased about 40 percent a year on average, and the installed capacity of wind turbines has doubled.

The dramatic growth of the wind and solar industries has led utilities to begin testing large-scale technologies capable of storing surplus clean electricity and delivering it on demand when sunlight and wind are in short supply.

Now a team of Stanford researchers has looked at the "energetic cost" of manufacturing batteries and other storage technologies for the electrical grid. At issue is whether renewable energy supplies, such as wind power and solar photovoltaics, produce enough energy to fuel both their own growth and the growth of the necessary energy storage industry.

Wind Energy Is Sustainable

"Whenever you build a new technology, you have to invest a large amount of energy up front," said Michael Dale, a research associate at Stanford. "Studies show that wind turbines and solar photovoltaic installations now produce more energy than they consume. The question is, how much additional grid-scale storage can the wind and solar industries afford and still remain net energy providers to the electrical grid?"

Wind technologies generate far more energy than they consume.

Writing in the March 19 [2014] online edition of the journal *Energy & Environmental Science*, Dale and his Stanford colleagues found that, from an energetic perspective, the wind industry can easily afford lots of storage, enough to provide more than three days of uninterrupted power. However, the study also revealed that the solar industry can afford only about 24 hours of energy storage. That's because it takes more energy to manufacture solar panels than wind turbines.

"We looked at the additional burden that would be placed on the solar and wind industries by concurrently building out batteries and other storage technologies," said Dale, the lead author of the study. "Our analysis shows that today's wind industry, even with a large amount of grid-scale storage, is energetically sustainable. We found that the solar industry can also achieve sustainable storage capacity by reducing the amount of energy that goes into making solar photovoltaics." Reducing energy inputs to battery manufacturing is also needed, he said.

Over the years, consumers have learned to expect electricity on demand from power plants that run on coal, natural gas or oil. But these fossil fuels, which provide reliable, around-the-clock energy, also emit megatons of greenhouse gas that contribute to global warming.

Wind and solar farms provide emissions-free energy, but only generate electricity when the wind blows or the sun shines. Surplus energy can be stored for later use, but today's electrical grid has little storage capacity, so other measures are used to balance electricity supply and demand.

In the study, the Stanford team considered a variety of storage technologies for the grid, including batteries and geologic systems, such as pumped hydroelectric storage. For the wind industry, the findings were very favorable.

"Wind technologies generate far more energy than they consume," Dale said. "Our study showed that wind actually produces enough surplus electricity to support up to 72 hours of either battery or geologic storage. This suggests that the industry could deploy enough storage to cope with three-day lulls in wind, common to many weather systems, and still provide net electricity to society."

The results were especially good for onshore wind turbines. "We found that onshore wind backed by three days of geologic storage can support annual growth rates of 100 percent—in other words, double in size each year—and still maintain an energy surplus," he said.

"These results are very encouraging," said study co-author Sally Benson, a professor of energy resources engineering and director of the Global Climate and Energy Project (GCEP) at Stanford. "They show that you could create a sustainable energy system that grows and maintains itself by combining wind and storage together. This depends on the growth rate of the industry, because the faster you grow, the more energy you need to build new turbines and batteries."

Solar and Other Considerations

For the solar industry, the Stanford team found that more work is needed to make grid-scale storage energetically sustainable. The study revealed that some solar technologies, such as single-crystal silicon cells, are growing so fast that they are net energy sinks—that is, they consume more power than they give back to the electrical grid. From an energetic standpoint, these industries "cannot support any level of storage," the study concluded.

"Our analysis showed that, from an energetic perspective, most photovoltaic technologies can only afford up to 24 hours of storage with an equal mix of battery and pumped hydropower," Dale said. "This suggests that solar photovoltaic systems could be deployed with enough storage to supply electricity at night, and the industry could still operate at a net energy surplus."

Although grid-scale storage of wind power might not be cost effective compared to buying power from the grid, it is energetically affordable, even with the wind industry growing at a double-digit pace.

One advantage of wind over solar power is that it has an enormous energy return on investment, Benson explained. "Within a few months, a wind turbine generates enough electricity to pay back all of the energy it took to build it," she said. "But some photovoltaics have an energy payback time of almost two years. To sustainably support grid-scale storage will require continued reductions in the amount of fossil fuel used to manufacture photovoltaic cells."

The Stanford team's primary focus was on the energetic cost of deploying storage on wind and solar farms. The researchers did not calculate how much energy would be required to build and replace grid-scale batteries every few years, nor did they consider the financial cost of building and installing large storage systems on the grid.

"People often ask, is storage a good or bad solution for intermittent renewable energy?" Benson said. "That question turns out to be way too simplistic. It's neither good nor bad. Although grid-scale storage of wind power might not be cost effective compared to buying power from the grid, it is energetically affordable, even with the wind industry growing at a double-digit pace.

"The solar industry needs to continue to reduce the amount of energy it needs to build photovoltaic modules before it can afford as much storage as wind can today."

7

Wind Energy Is Not Reliable

Alex Fitzsimmons

Alex Fitzsimmons is a policy associate at the Institute for Energy Research.

A polar vortex in January 2014 created a greater need for energy across the United States. As demand rose, wind production was not able to keep up. Nuclear and coal energy, which does not rely on the weather, is a much more predictable source of energy. Nuclear and coal energy production must continue to reduce the risk of blackouts during peak demand. Wind energy is not reliable enough to meet the needs of the population.

Reliable energy sources and a diverse fuel mix are integral to maintaining America's electric grid and keeping the lights on. The electric grid must be carefully balanced at all times so that supply matches demand or otherwise blackout would occur. This means that the grid needs reliable sources of generation to keep supply and demand matched at all times. New data on the polar vortex that swept the nation in January [2014] show how difficult this can be and highlight the perils of government policies designed to replace reliable energy sources with intermittent ones.

What we already know: as temperatures dropped across the country in early January [2014], the cold weather increased demand for natural gas used both for home heating and for gas-fired electric generators. Surging demand, combined with constrained pipeline capacity, led to spiking prices and inadequate natural gas supplies (some customers had their natural gas service interrupted).

To meet the increased electricity demand and prevent power outages, grid operators relied on coal, nuclear, and even petroleum generating units. Wind energy, on the other hand, actually performed worst when it was needed most, according to new data from the PJM Interconnection. This further debunks the wind industry's claim that wind energy plays an important role in keeping the lights on during low temperature events.

PJM's data also highlight a fatal flaw in EPA's [Environmental Protection Agency] proposed ban on coal-fired power plants. EPA assumes that no new coal plants will be built in the foreseeable future, but EPA failed to see that the problems caused by constrained pipeline capacity and a dwindling number of coal-fired power plants. EPA is causing coal facilities to shutter while subsidized and ill-timed wind power continues to force the premature closure of nuclear plants, creating an absence of reliable alternatives to natural gas and leaving Americans vulnerable to future and more dramatic price shocks.

Unlike nuclear, coal, and natural gas, wind is an inherently variable energy source whose output is dictated by Mother Nature, not by consumer demand, prices, or emergency orders.

Wind Choked When It Was Needed Most

The PJM Interconnection is a regional grid operator that serves all or parts of 13 Northeastern, Mid Atlantic, and Midwestern states and the District of Columbia. Coal, nuclear, and natural gas together comprise 75 percent of the PJM's electrical generating capacity (41 percent, 18 percent, and 16 percent, respectively). Wind energy accounts for less than one half of one percent of installed capacity.

In early January [2014], the polar vortex increased energy demand and drove up natural gas prices. As temperatures plunged and demand rose, nuclear and coal generators picked up the slack. In contrast, according to PJM data, wind energy generation dropped from 4 gigawatts (GW) on January 6 to less than 2 GW during demand peaks on January 7 and less than 800 megawatts (MW) on January 9. . . .

While wind production declined steadily as demand rose, nuclear provided a reliable supply of generation to meet demand. Between January 4 and 8, the nation's nuclear fleet operated at more than 95 percent of capacity, according to the Nuclear Energy Institute.

To illustrate the reliability differences between nuclear and wind, consider this. During the polar vortex, AWEA [American Wind Energy Association] claimed "wind energy provided massive quantities of extremely valuable electricity when grid operators needed it most," particularly in Texas, where wind made the "critical difference" in preventing outages. Far from providing "massive quantities" of energy, IER's analysis found that wind energy operated at just 17 percent of its total capacity in Texas during the polar vortex. AWEA congratulates its industry for production at 17 percent of capacity while nuclear operating at 95 percent capacity goes unrecognized.

PJM's data demonstrate that wind energy cannot be relied on to provide significant amounts of energy during peak demand. Unlike nuclear, coal, and natural gas, wind is an inherently variable energy source whose output is dictated by Mother Nature, not by consumer demand, prices, or emergency orders. This is why ERCOT, the Texas grid operator, counts only 8.7 percent of its wind capacity toward its reserve level.

Onerous Regulations Threaten the Electric Grid

The polar vortex shows the value of reliable energy to the electric grid. It also highlights the perils of government regulations designed to undermine reliable energy. The Nuclear Regulatory Commission put 38 nuclear units on a retirement list due to a number of factors, including regulatory costs. If all 38 at-risk units were prematurely retired, about one-third of the U.S. nuclear fleet would be shut down. Compounding this problem is the fact that few new nuclear units are scheduled to come on line to replace existing units. This means nuclear power's contribution to the U.S. energy mix is likely to shrink.

Regulations are also forcing many coal plants into early retirement. EPA regulations will shutter 60 gigawatts, or 20 percent, of the nation's coal-fired generating capacity by 2016, coinciding with the first year of enforcement for EPA's Mercury Air Toxics Standards (MATS). But that's not all, this summer EPA will propose carbon dioxide emission restrictions on existing coal-fired power plants. According to the Energy Information Administration, coal currently provides nearly 40 percent of America's electricity, but this will decrease under EPA's regulatory onslaught.

> *Wind energy, unlike nuclear, coal, and natural gas, cannot be relied on to provide significant amounts of energy when it is needed most.*

Reliable energy sources like nuclear and coal are needed to maintain the integrity of the electric grid, especially during peak demand. Onerous regulations aimed at shuttering reliable energy sources threaten to undermine grid reliability. In testimony before Congress in December, Philip Moeller, a commissioner for the Federal Energy Regulatory Commission (FERC), warned that the Midwest could experience rolling blackouts in 2016 due a shortfall of coal reserves after the MATS rule takes effect. Given FERC's central role in ensuring the reliability of the nation's power grid, policymakers should take notice when Commissioners signal that the grid is facing real reliability issues. Commissioner Moeller did not mention wind energy as a solution to the shortfall.

Reliable energy sources and a diverse fuel mix are essential to the electric grid. When natural gas prices spiked in early January amid record low temperatures, grid operators leaned on nuclear and coal to prevent power outages. These sources performed admirably, with nuclear operating at an average capacity of more than 95 percent.

Wind energy, unlike nuclear, coal, and natural gas, cannot be relied on to provide significant amounts of energy when it is needed most. In fact, wind energy actually became less reliable to the PJM grid operator during the polar vortex as temperatures dropped and demand soared. Even in Texas, where the wind industry claimed victory for the "massive quantities" of wind energy supplied to the grid during the polar vortex, wind energy operated at just 17 percent of its total capacity.

Onerous regulations imperil America's supply of reliable energy, which in turn threatens grid reliability. EPA regulations, especially the MATS rule, will shutter 20 percent of U.S. coal-fired generating capacity by 2016 and more will close with EPA's carbon dioxide restrictions. Meanwhile, almost 40 percent of the U.S. nuclear fleet has been put on a list of potential retirements. The polar vortex provides further evidence that government policies should support reliable energy, not undermine grid reliability. Failure to change course will only result in more of the same—price shocks, supply interruptions, and unreliable power.

8

Wind Energy Is Economical

Michael Goggin

Michael Goggin is director of research at the American Wind Energy Association.

As proven by the extreme winter the United States experienced in 2014, newer wind turbines create energy that is more reliable than conventional forms of energy. Wind energy was able to meet US demand even while more traditional forms of energy, such as coal plants, failed. Wind energy also saves consumers money by replacing more costly energy sources. Wind is an important part of the diverse supply of energy needed for preserving US energy stability.

Wind energy plays a critical role in providing American consumers with low-cost, stably-priced, reliable electricity.

Wind energy repeatedly proved its reliability and value this winter by protecting consumers across the U.S. from fuel shortages and extreme spikes in energy prices. In region after region, wind energy output was consistently strong as extreme cold drove record demand for electricity use at the same time that the cold caused failures at many conventional power plants. These events compellingly illustrated that all energy sources fail from time to time, so a diverse mix of resources that includes wind energy is critical for reliability and for protecting consumers from price spikes. Here are a few examples from this winter:

Early on January 6 [2014], the Nebraska Public Power District met record winter electricity demand with wind energy providing about 13 percent of its electricity. The utility explained in a press release that "Nebraskans benefit from NPPD's diverse portfolio of generating resources. Using a combination of fuels means we deliver electricity using the lowest cost resources while maintaining high reliability for our customers." The utility also noted that "NPPD did not operate its natural gas generation because the fuel costs were up more than 300 percent over typical prices."

Later on January 6 [2014], the grid operator for the Mid-Atlantic and Great Lakes states had 3,000 MW of wind output when it faced its most severe challenge of the winter due to the unexpected failure of 20 percent of its conventional power plants in the cold. On January 22 and 23, the region's wind output was again above 3,000 MW, saving consumers millions as the grid operator saw electricity and natural gas prices skyrocket to 10–50 times normal due to another bout of extreme cold.

On an average annual basis, wind energy produces more than 25 percent of the electricity in Iowa and South Dakota, 12 percent or more in nine states, and five percent or more in 17 states.

Finally, when "a shortage of natural gas triggered by extreme cold weather" hit California on February 6 [2014], wind energy provided the state with around 2,000 MW at the time of peak demand, with wind output above 2,500 MW for most of the rest of the evening, allowing the grid operator to avoid calling an energy emergency alert.

Wind Energy Meets Production Needs

Nationwide in January [2014], wind energy produced a record 18 million Megawatt-hours, the highest monthly total in history, enough electricity to power the equivalent of 20 million typical U.S. homes at average usage rates. Wind energy provided 4.86 percent of all electricity produced in the month, a remarkable feat given that the sustained record cold caused January to set a new record for winter electricity demand.

On an average annual basis, wind energy produces more than 25 percent of the electricity in Iowa and South Dakota, 12 percent or more in nine states, and five percent or more in 17 states. In certain hours, wind has supplied more than 60 percent of the electricity on the main utility system in Colorado, and the main grid in Texas has gone above 39 percent, all without any reliability problems.

Thanks to technological advances, today's wind turbines use sophisticated controls and power electronics to provide many grid reliability services as well as or better than conventional power plants. Because changes in wind energy output are gradual and predictable, while the failures of conventional power plants occur instantaneously and without warning, it is far more expensive to back up conventional power plants than wind energy.

The Mid-Atlantic grid operator recently concluded that even if its use of wind energy increased by a factor of seven, or 28,000 MW, the need for reserves would only increase by 340 MW, about $1/10^{th}$ of the 3,350 MW of reserves it holds 24/7 in case a large conventional power plant breaks down.

Last month, the American Wind Energy Association (AWEA) released a report demonstrating how wind and the Production Tax Credit are compatible with well-functioning wholesale power markets, and thoroughly debunking claims made by Exelon, the country's largest owner of merchant power plants. Our report showed that negative prices occur at Exelon's nuclear plants at a fraction of the rate claimed by Exelon, that the majority of those negative prices are actually caused by the inability of Exelon's nuclear plants to change their output in response to transmission outages and other factors unrelated to wind, that the rare occurrences of negative prices are relegated to remote pockets of the grid where they have little to no impact on other power plants, and that negative prices are rapidly being eliminated anyway by new transmission lines.

We have since conducted additional analysis demonstrating that low fossil fuel prices and declining electricity demand are having a nearly 1500 times larger impact on the economics of Exelon's nuclear power plants than occurrences of negative prices.

Wind energy is saving consumers money by displacing more expensive forms of energy. This is a market-driven mechanism that occurs for all low-variable-cost sources of generation, including nuclear. This impact is not caused by the renewable tax credit, but rather occurs due to wind's zero fuel cost. Wind's locked-in, zero fuel cost also plays an important role in protecting consumers from increases in the price of other fuels, whether those are short-term spikes caused by extreme weather as we saw this winter, or long-term uncertainty about the price of other fuels.

9

Wind Turbines Are Wiping Out Bird Populations

Robert Johns

Robert Johns is the director of public relations at the American Bird Conservancy.

The life expectancy for several species of birds, including eagles and raptors, has gone down as the presence of wind turbines has increased. Poor siting and increasingly larger turbines could put over a million birds at risk annually. There needs to be mandatory standards for wind turbines so that birds will be protected.

A new study shows that in spite of updated designs, U.S. wind turbines are killing hundreds of thousands of birds annually—a number that may balloon to about 1.4 million per year by 2030, when the ongoing industry expansion being encouraged by the federal government is expected to be fully implemented.

Bird Collision Study

The findings were issued in a new study by scientists at the Smithsonian Institution Migratory Bird Center (SMBC), the U.S. Fish and Wildlife Service (FWS) and Oklahoma State University (OSU), published in the December issue of the journal *Biological Conservation* and authored by Scott Loss (OSU), Tom Will (FWS), and Peter Marra (SMBC).

The study, "Estimates of bird collision mortality at wind facilities in the contiguous United States," was based on a review of 68 studies that met rigorous inclusion criteria and data derived from 58 bird mortality estimates contained in those studies. The studies represented both peer-reviewed and unpublished industry reports and extracted data to systematically estimate bird collision mortality and mortality correlates.

"The life expectancy for eagles and all raptors just took a big hit. Clearly, when you look at this study and you consider the new 30-year eagle take permits just announced by the Department of Interior, this is a bad month for this country's iconic birds," said Dr. Michael Hutchins, National Coordinator of American Bird Conservancy's (ABC) Bird Smart Wind Energy campaign.

According to George Fenwick, President of ABC: "This study by top scientists says that hundreds of thousands of birds are being killed by the wind industry now, and that the number will escalate dramatically if we continue to do what we have been doing. The biggest impediment to reducing those impacts continues to be wind industry siting and operating guidelines that are only followed on a voluntary basis. No other energy industry gets to pick and choose where they put their facilities and decide how they are going to operate in a manner unconstrained by federal regulation."

Poorly sited and operated wind projects pose a serious threat to birds, especially birds of prey such as Bald Eagles, Golden Eagles, hawks, and owls.

"The industry has been saying for some time that bird mortality would be reduced with the new turbines compared to the older, lattice structures. According to this study, that does not appear to be the case," Hutchins pointed out, since the study excluded data from wind developments using older designs.

Wildlife Protection Violations

"The status quo is legally, as well as environmentally, unsustainable," Hutchins said further. "The federal government is seeking to promote an energy sector in a manner that is in violation of one of the premier federal wildlife protection statutes. In December 2011, we formally petitioned the Department of the Interior to develop mandatory regulations that will safeguard wildlife and reward responsible wind energy development. We continue to believe that is the solution."

A coalition of more than 60 groups has called for mandatory standards and bird-smart principles in the siting and operation of wind energy installations. The coalition represents a broad cross-section of respected national and local groups. In addition, 20,000 scientists, ornithologists, conservationists, and other concerned citizens have shown their support for mandatory standards for the wind industry.

According to ABC, poorly sited and operated wind projects pose a serious threat to birds, especially birds of prey such as Bald Eagles, Golden Eagles, hawks, and owls; endangered and threatened species such as California Condors and Whooping Cranes; and species of special conservation concern such as the Bicknell's Thrush, Cerulean Warbler, Tricolored Blackbird, Sprague's Pipit, and Long-billed Curlew.

One particularly interesting finding of the new study concerned the height of turbines. The scientists found that bird collision mortality increased significantly with increasing hub height. Across a range of turbine heights from 36 to 80 meters, the study predicts a staggering tenfold increase in bird mortality. This is especially important because the study identifies an apparent trend toward increased turbine height. Further, the study states: "This estimate (1.4 million) assumes that average wind turbine height will not increase. Installation of increasingly larger turbines could result in a greater amount of mortality." Such an eventuality may be likely given that a Department of Energy report found that the average turbine hub height of U.S. wind turbines has increased 50 percent between 1998 and 2012.

The report offered several additional key observations about wind energy and bird mortality:

- The mortality rate at wind farms in California was dramatically higher than anywhere else. According to the study: "We estimate that 46.4% of total mortality at monopole wind turbines occurs in California, 23.1% occurs in the Great Plains, 18.8% occurs in the East, and 11.6% occurs in the West."

- Failure to consider species-specific risks may result in relatively high rates of mortality for some bird species even if total mortality is relatively low.

- Annual mortality estimates derived from a partial year of sampling may substantially underestimate mortality. Pre-construction studies should be conducted for at least one entire year prior to wind facility siting decisions.

- The fatality records in the study identified at least 218 species of birds killed at wind energy installations.

- Conclusions about collision rates and impacts of collisions on bird populations are tentative because most of the mortality data is in industry reports that are not subjected to peer review or available to the public.

- Pre-construction assessment of collision risk at proposed wind facilities has been unreliable with no clear link documented between predicted risk levels and post-construction mortality rates.

"A key issue that was illustrated in this study, and one that we continue to have great concerns about, is data transparency and availability. While some companies may do the right thing and collect bird mortality data and make it available, others may not, especially if it is not in their economic interest," Hutchins added.

The new study comes just after the Department of Justice announced a settlement on the prosecution of Duke Energy's wind developments in Wyoming in connection with the deaths of 14 Golden Eagles and 149 other protected birds. That first-ever settlement resulted in $1 million in fines and mitigation actions and was the first prosecution of a wind company in connection with bird mortality.

10

Wind Energy Should Not Be Exempt from the Endangered Species Act

Paul Driessen

Paul Driessen is the author of Eco-Imperialism: Green Power— Black Death *and senior policy advisor for the Committee for a Constructive Tomorrow.*

Wind energy has many environmental drawbacks and is not sustainable. Although the US Fish and Wildlife Service has prosecuted other industries for harming wildlife, wind energy companies are not held responsible for massive wildlife deaths. Not only are energy companies given a free pass when it comes to wildlife, their operations are heavily subsidized by the government.

"Gleaming white wind turbines generating carbon-free electricity carpet chaparral-covered ridges and march down into valleys of Joshua trees." Such is "the future" of American energy, *not* "the oil rigs planted helter-skelter in [nearby] citrus groves."

So reads a recent *Forbes* article. But Wind vs. Bird by Todd Woody also raises concern about the fate of a 300-megawatt "green" turbine project threatening California condors, a species just coming back from the edge of extinction. The project might be cancelled as a result.

Indeed, the U.S. Fish & Wildlife Service (FWS) has asked Kern County to "exercise extreme caution" in approving projects in the Tehapachi area, because of potential threats to condors. The "conundrum will force some hard choices about the balance we are willing to strike between obtaining clean energy and preserving wild things," the article suggested. Hopefully, it concluded, new "avian radar units" will be able to detect condors and automatically shut down turbines when one approaches.

Wind Energy and Wildlife

All Americans hope condors will not be sliced and diced by giant Cuisinarts. But most of us are puzzled that so few "environmentalists" and FWS "caretakers" express concern about the countless bald and golden eagles, hawks, falcons, vultures, ducks, geese, bats, and other rare, threatened, endangered and common flying creatures imperiled by turbine blades.

And many of us get downright angry at the selective way endangered species and other wildlife laws are applied—leaving wind turbine operators free to exact their carnage, while harassing and punishing oil companies and citizens.

This is hardly a new issue. In his August 1997 essay for the Cato Institute, "Renewable Energy: Not Cheap, Not 'Green,'" Robert Bradley documented the "avian mortality" problem before taking to task one of the nation's leading (anti-) energy environmentalists who was just a car ride away from well-documented windpower carnage:

> Wind power's land disturbance, noise, and unsightly turbines also present environmental drawbacks, at least from the perspective of some if not many mainstream environmentalists. Yet at least one well-known environmental group has a double standard when considering wind power versus other energy options. In testimony before the California Public Utilities Commission (CPUC), Ralph Cavanagh of the Natural Resources Defense Council argued against open-

ing the electricity industry to competition and customer choice because of the "development of significant new transmission and distribution lines to link buyers and sellers of power. In addition to the visual blight of additional power lines on the landscape, these corridors can displace threatened or endangered species."

Bradley continues:

Yet Altamont Pass's 7,000 turbines (located near Cavanagh's San Francisco office) have a record of sizable avian mortality, large land-use requirements, disturbing noise, and "visual blight." The irony of visual blight was not lost on environmental philosopher Roderick Nash, who, referring to the Santa Barbara environmentalists, asked, "If offshore rigs offend, can a much greater number of windmills be any better?"

A double standard . . . and for a long time.

Wind turbine companies, officers, and employees . . . are immune from prosecution, fines or imprisonment, regardless of how many rare, threatened, endangered, or migratory birds and bats they kill.

In 2011, following a million-dollar, 45-day helicopter search for dead birds in North Dakota oil fields, U.S. Attorney Timothy Purdon prosecuted seven oil and gas companies for inadvertently killing 28 mallard ducks, flycatchers, and other common birds that were found dead in or near uncovered waste pits. Under the Migratory Bird Treaty Act, the companies and their executive officers faced fines of up to $15,000 per bird, plus six months in prison. (They eventually agreed to plead guilty and pay $1,000 per bird.)

Also in 2011, a FWS agent charged an 11-year-old Virginia girl with illegally possessing a baby woodpecker that the girl had rescued from a housecat, even though she intended to release the bird after ensuring it was OK. The threatened $535 fine was finally dropped, after the FWS was deservedly ridiculed in the media.

The mere possession of an eagle feather by a non-Indian can result in fines and imprisonment, even if the feather came from a bird butchered by a wind turbine: up to $100,000, a year in prison or both for a first offense. Poisoning or otherwise killing common bats that have nested in one's attic can cost homeowners thousands of dollars in fines.

Windpower Is Immune to Prosecution

Wind turbine companies, officers, and employees, however, are immune from prosecution, fines or imprisonment, regardless of how many rare, threatened, endangered, or migratory birds and bats they kill. In fact, FWS data show that wind turbines slaughter some 400,000 birds every year. If "helter-skelter" applies to any energy source, it is wind turbines, reflecting their Charles Manson [convicted serial killer] effect on birds.

The hypocritical [President Barack] Obama-[US Attorney Tim] Purdon-FWS policy exists solely to protect, promote, and advance an anti-hydrocarbon agenda that is increasingly at odds with environmental, scientific, economic, job-creation and public opinion reality—and to safeguard wind turbines that survive solely because of government mandates, taxpayer subsidies ... and exemptions from laws that rule, penalize, and terrorize the rest of us.

Even if avian radar and turbine shutdown systems do eventually work, should they be limited to condors? Shouldn't they be required for eagles and falcons—and for hawks, ducks, flycatchers, bats, and other protected species? For geese, to prevent a repeat of the December 7, 2011, massacre of numerous snow geese by wind turbines along upstate New York Route 190, as reported by a motorist?

Why aren't wind developers and permitting authorities required to consider the lost economic benefits of butchered birds and bats, which do so much to control rats and insects that carry diseases and destroy crops?

Of course, even condor protection alone would likely limit affected turbine electricity output to 10% or 20% of rated capacity, instead of their current 30% average. Adding other protected species would drive nearly all actual wind turbine electricity output down below 5%—making the turbines virtually worthless, and driving the exorbitant cost of wind energy even higher.

Put bluntly, wind energy is unsustainable. It kills unconscionable numbers of bats, raptors, and other birds.

But why should wind turbines be above the law? Why should we even worry about reducing their electricity output?

America's environmentalists, legislators, judges, and bureaucrats have already made hundreds of millions of acres of resource-rich land off limits—and rendered centuries of oil, gas, coal, uranium, geothermal, and other energy unavailable. The Environmental Protection Agency's anti-coal aero-pollution rules, intense opposition to the Keystone pipeline, and looming restrictions on hydraulic fracturing for natural gas are already further impairing electricity and other energy availability and reliability.

This government-imposed energy deprivation is already driving families into energy poverty and sending more jobs overseas.

Put bluntly, wind energy is unsustainable. It kills unconscionable numbers of bats, raptors, and other birds. It requires billions in perpetual subsidies—and billions more for (mostly) gas-fired backup generators. It impacts millions of acres of scenic, wildlife, and agricultural land—and uses vast amounts of raw materials, whose extraction and processing further impairs global land, air, and water quality. Its expensive, unreliable electricity kills two jobs for every one supposedly created.

A far more rational public policy would cut the *crony* out of capitalism and *double* out of standards. Fair field, no favor.

So be it that wind turbines would fall by the wayside and consumers support conventional energies to generate reliable, affordable, sustainable electricity. Consumers? That is all of us. Energy planners? That is a small number of them.

11

Outer Banks Offshore Wind Farm Gets Blowback

Scott Harper

Scott Harper covered environmental issues for the Virginian-Pilot *until his death in 2013.*

Community leaders in the barrier island region of North Carolina are concerned that an offshore wind farm visible from land would hurt the tourist industry and ruin the landscape. Although building farther from land would protect the view and also avoid underwater relics, it would also add additional cost to the project. Despite numerous protests, many realize that wind turbines in the area of the barrier islands are probably unavoidable.

Most Outer Banks visitors know a trip to the beach is sure to include one constant: wind, and lots of it. The kind that turns umbrellas into tumbleweeds and drives sand into eyes, hair, food, swimsuits.

The barrier islands are seemingly always windy, as they jut naked and exposed into the Atlantic Ocean. No wonder, then, that the U.S. government has chosen a huge swath of water just off the Outer Banks as a potential home for an offshore wind farm in the near future.

The site recommended by the Bureau of Ocean Energy Management would extend along some of the most popular beaches, starting around Pea Island and heading north past

Nags Head, Kill Devil Hills, Kitty Hawk, Southern Shores and Duck and ending off Corolla, just below the Virginia border—a 45-mile stretch.

Troubling to most of these communities, however, is that the government would allow giant wind turbines to be built 6 miles from shore, easily visible on most days.

Community leaders fear that hundreds of clean-energy turbines would ruin the laid-back allure of the Outer Banks and harm the lucrative tourist industry, the backbone of the local economy.

Similarly, the National Park Service has expressed concern about turbines ruining scenic views and dark night skies from the Cape Hatteras National Seashore and the Wright Brothers National Memorial. The turbines would require blinking safety lights at night.

No one can say for sure how many windmills might be built—planning still is under way—estimates indicate that at full capacity, more than 2,000 could fit into the assigned area, which covers more than 1,000 square nautical miles.

The Kitty Hawk Town Council passed a resolution earlier this year opposing any turbines within miles of the coast.

"Once those turbines go in, that's it, you're stuck with them for better or for worse," said Gary Perry, mayor pro tem of the town of Kitty Hawk, who also was a member of an offshore energy task force under former Gov. Beverly Perdue.

"Ideally, we'd like no offshore wind in our tourist zone," Perry added. "But we also recognize offshore wind energy is probably inevitable, and that its development will likely occur. We just want to have a say in where it goes."

To that end, the Kitty Hawk Town Council passed a resolution earlier this year opposing any turbines within miles of the coast. Instead, the town urged the government to push back its starting line to at least 20 miles. At that distance, the windmills, each more than 400 feet tall, could barely be seen, if at all. . . .

The Kitty Hawk council also balked at a test proposal last year from a Spanish wind developer and defense conglomerate Northrop Grumman. They wanted to erect three turbines a half-mile from shore—not unlike what had been approved in the Chesapeake Bay off Cape Charles on Virginia's Eastern Shore. Both projects, though, eventually died.

The wind area recommended off the Outer Banks is within miles of where the government suggested one be set off Virginia's coast. That site is about seven times smaller than the Outer Banks zone and would be at least 23 miles due east Virginia Beach. . . .

Eight companies have expressed an interest in buying leases within the Virginia wind zone, while five indicated a desire to Outer Banks leases. One of those active in both states is Dominion Power, Virginia's largest electric utility.

There are plenty of wind farms operating on land in the United States, but none on water.

Guy Chapman, Dominion's director of alternative energy technologies, said acquiring leases off Virginia and North Carolina seems logical on several fronts, with the potential that clean electricity generated at the sites could be carried to land and processed at the same place, probably in Virginia Beach.

Chapman also said Dominion is willing to develop wind about 12 miles from land, where a turbine "would look like the knuckle on the back of your hand, even on a clear day."

While Dominion is willing to move farther back, the Virginia Port Authority [VPA] is encouraging the government to stay closer to land.

In written comments, the VPA said more than 5,000 commercial vessels access the ports of Virginia and Baltimore via the Chesapeake Bay and that most of these trips go directly through the proposed Outer Banks wind zone.

The VPA's director of environmental affairs, Heather Wood, wrote that the government, to avert a potentially dangerous traffic jam, should "only grant leases in the western most portions" of the wind area—meaning, those closest to shore.

There are plenty of wind farms operating on land in the United States, but none on water. That stands in stark contrast to most European countries and in China, where offshore turbines today spin a steady dose of clean energy—but often at expensive rates requiring subsidies to make them competitive with traditional sources.

On a recent day in Kitty Hawk, the beaches were crowded with students fresh out of school and adults lounging near the surf. A stiff wind, of course, was blowing.

Few knew about the government's proposal to develop a wind farm miles away, and most seemed stunned by the news.

"Right out there?! Are you kidding?" said Mary Klingsbury, visiting Kitty Hawk from Pennsylvania with her family. "Why so close?"

Others said the turbines simply represent changing times and the need for clean energy. They said construction would not bother them.

"I think it might be cool to see them out there," said Samuel Burns, a rising college sophomore from Maryland's Eastern Shore, who was throwing a football with friends. "It's something we have to do."

North Carolina Gov. Pat McCrory seems to agree with Burns—at least on wind power.

McCrory, a Republican, touts a report from the National Renewable Energy Laboratory that estimates offshore energy resources off Carolina could generate $22 billion in economic activity and create as many as 10,000 jobs.

But McCrory also endorses oil and gas drilling off the coast—a position that Burns and his friends said they do not support. Most Outer Banks residents also oppose drilling, according to several community leaders.

"Development of North Carolina's offshore wind energy resources is not just good for this state's economy," McCrory wrote in January to the Bureau of Ocean Energy Management, "but it will continue to fulfill work toward an 'all of the above' strategy to move our nation toward greater energy independence."

Officials estimate it could take at least another five years to negotiate, study, permit and construct wind farms off the Carolina coast. Virginia is moving faster, with a federal auction for offshore wind leases expected as soon as this summer.

12

Offshore Wind Farms Could Attract Tourists

Christina Albrecht, Andreas Wagner, and Kerstin Wesselmann

Christina Albrecht and Kerstin Wesselmann are management assistants at the German Offshore Wind Energy Foundation. Andreas Wagner is the managing director at the Foundation.

While many are fearful that offshore wind turbines could have a detrimental impact on tourism, both because of interference with boat traffic and interrupted views, research suggests the opposite. Offshore wind farms could actually attract tourists who wish to visit and learn about the turbines, who enjoy the entertainment value of viewing the turbines from shore, and who want their travel to reflect the values they hold regarding clean energy and the environment. Additionally, the jobs created with wind farms bring additional prosperity to the area, making it more attractive for tourists.

Due to the importance of tourism for coastal regions, locals will have a number of fears and prejudices regarding offshore wind energy. [G.] Hilligweg and [S.] Kull summarize possible disadvantages as damage to image due to disturbing emotions. Concerning the offshore wind industry, this includes impacts on the landscape, use of sea space, noise, shadow flickering and impacts on tourism due to ship collisions.

Christina Albrecht, Andreas Wagner, and Kerstin Wesselmann, "Chapter 2: Offshore Wind Energy—Impacts on Regional Tourism: Fears, Prejudices and Benefits," *The Impact of Offshore Wind Energy on Tourism: Good Practices and Perspectives for the South Baltic Region*, April 2013. pp. 12-17. Copyright © 2013 Stiftung Offshore Wind Energie. All rights reserved. Reprinted with permission.

Since tourism depends on an attractive environment, locals fear that impacts on the landscape, e.g. the agglomeration of several and/or very big wind turbines, might negatively affect the leisure zone. This again could result in a loss of recreational value and less demand for the tourism area. Important factors are therefore the location of turbines and their visibility from shore. However, according to Hilligweg and Kull, only 9% of interview respondents are disturbed by offshore wind energy farms regardless of their position. More than half of the respondents would not even be disturbed if the wind energy farm would be visible.

The encroachment on an area by offshore wind farms, and the traffic laws and safety regulations that follow, result in impacts on ship and boat tourism.

General Acceptance

A study on the wind farms Nysted, 10 kilometres from shore, and Horns Rev, some 14–20 kilometres from shore, undertaken by the Danish Energy Authority, showed that "local and national populations are generally positive towards wind farms. On the other hand there is also a significant willingness to pay to locate future wind farms at distances where visual effects on the coastal landscape are reduced." Apparently "more than 40% of the respondents in both the Horns Rev and Nysted samples stated that they would prefer future wind farms to be moved out of sight. In the national sample more than half of the respondents stated that they would prefer wind farms to be moved out of sight." In addition "more than 70% of local and national respondents stated that they would prefer larger and fewer farms" over "wind farms in several small groups." Identification of the visual impacts before construction of a wind farm, together with public involvement, can help to lower fears regarding destruction of the landscape.

However this effect is especially relevant where offshore wind farms are located nearshore or not very distant from the shore (mainly in Denmark and Sweden).

Contrary to Denmark, most German offshore projects are planned and implemented outside the 12 nautical mile zone in the exclusive economic zone where they cannot or only hardly be seen from the shore. The transmission of electricity to the load centres inland is another factor potentially impacting the landscape since an increased number of overhead lines might become necessary. An alternative would be the hauling of underground cables, but this might be more cost intensive.

In order to reduce negative impacts due to aesthetics of offshore wind farms and overhead lines, they could be constructed in a manner which make them suitable to the landscape and represent a landmark. The Federal Ministry of Transport, Building and Urban Development in Germany argues for the capacity of building culture to emphasize positive effects and minimize negative impacts, and therefore create buildings which engender pride and a desire for their conservation, and which become a part of the region. A good practice example in this context is the unique shape of the Middelgrunden offshore wind farm in Denmark. In addition, advertising could be used to emphasize the aesthetics of offshore wind farms in a positive manner, since the opinion of the observer is ultimately always subjective. The German Energy Agency regards an offshore wind farm as a neutral structure. Most critical for its acceptance is not the fact of its visibility, but the associations it elicits in the viewer. Therefore a good communication strategy is a crucial factor before and during the construction of offshore wind farms, since the main problem concerning their acceptance is a lack of information. It is important to treat existing fears seriously, to alleviate them, and to draw attention to benefits as well the disadvantages. In addition, the possibilities and limits of civic participation and/or involvement should be openly communicated. The visibility and accessibility of the responsible authorities, as well as the organisation in charge of project execution, should be guaranteed throughout the entire project's duration.

Fears for Boat Tourism

Use of sea space might pose a problem for boat tourism. The encroachment on an area by offshore wind farms, and the traffic laws and safety regulations that follow, result in impacts on ship and boat tourism. An area previously freely accessible is now restricted for shipping and boat traffic. To which extent a transit through offshore wind farm areas is possible depends on safety issues and its ease of access. Examples from Denmark, where transit through offshore wind energy farms is possible via certain routes, showed that sea usage due to offshore wind farms did not have any negative impacts on boat traffic. On the contrary, the offshore wind farm Nysted was regarded by sailors as an inducement to choose that route over others. In Germany, it is allowed to navigate as close as 500 meters to an offshore wind farm. However, it is not allowed to cross it by boat (except installation and service vessels). For example, amateur sailors will be able to reach the offshore wind farm Riffgat in the North Sea easily from the nearby island of Borkum.

Despite all the fears and prejudices, offshore wind energy has numerous benefits for tourism regions.

Noise and shadow flickering only affect ship and boat traffic in close proximity to the offshore wind farm, as they are not perceivable in the coastal areas. Thus minimal impact results from noise and shadow flickering in offshore wind farms. A higher acoustic emission only arises temporarily during the construction phase. Due to the rebound effect under water, this has greater significance for the maritime environment than it does for tourists. A large amount of ecological research has been initiated in Germany to develop strategies for noise mitigation during the construction phase.

Another fear is the risk of ship collisions, and the associated potential leakage of harmful substances, which potentially could have enduring negative effects on the environment, and therefore on tourism. In a study by [G.] Hübner and [J.] Pohl, inhabitants and tourists in four coastal regions of Germany were asked whether or not construction of the offshore wind farms had led to the impacts they had feared. During the workshops held for the locals, the main issue was always their fear of possible ship collision and its impacts. Despite statutory license regulations, locals criticized the close proximity of some offshore wind farms to sea-lanes with intensive traffic. Hübner and Pohl further state that the participants of the workshops were particularly critical of the fact that human failure, which is the most frequent cause of ship collisions, was not among the criteria for the approval certification. In addition, their research showed that the fear of ship collisions is bigger for wind farms in close proximity to the coast. The participants of the workshops called for compulsory pilots, control of shipping traffic, as well as—in the event of a ship collision—a sufficient number of local towboats. According to ARCADIS, there are no reliable methods to predict the likelihood of such an occurrence. However it is not only in the interest of the tourism industry, but also of the offshore wind energy industry, to attach a significant value to environmental protection and nature conservation. This is due to the fact that an ecological disaster would have enduring negative impacts on the industry's image. Therefore the offshore wind industry will do everything to avoid such an event.

A number of examples demonstrate that these fears and prejudices which arise prior to the construction of offshore wind farms, are mostly unjustified. In most cases, is was possible to incorporate the offshore wind energy project into the local tourism concept, and several representative studies verified that there was no decrease in the number of tourists after construction of an offshore wind farm. The assumption that tourists might stay away due to the existence of offshore wind farms is more a subjective fear than a measurable fact. The research of Hübner and Pohl showed that the fears held by locals ahead of construction were mostly eliminated after completion of the wind farms.

In addition to the obvious benefits stemming from attractions and values, the offshore wind energy industry spawns regional value creation.

Benefits to Tourism

Despite all the fears and prejudices, offshore wind energy has numerous benefits for tourism regions. Several of them are summarized in Hilligweg and Kull's category better image due to the value of experiencing entertainment. This includes the items "fascination with technology", "event character", as well as "contribution to active environmental protection". Another benefit is the general attractiveness of the region due to its prosperity.

According to the authors, a fascination with technology could lead to an increased number of visitors and day-trippers. Hübner and Pohl also state that the locals' curiosity about offshore wind energy is based on the fascination with its technology. In addition, the German Energy Agency finds that the technical aspects related to offshore wind energy are a fascinating subject, which can turn into a distinctive segment of the tourism industry. Apart from the highly impressive wind turbines, sea ports, construction sites and jack-up vessels offer much to see. A good example is the "Tour de Wind" sightseeing tour in Bremerhaven, which connects 20 stations related to onshore and especially offshore wind energy.

Hilligweg and Kull state that the promotion of offshore wind energy might create added value for a region by providing entertainment experiences. An edutainment event can give background information on offshore wind energy, linking it with entertainment and adventure. Offshore wind energy therefore has an event character. Further attractions, for instance an information centre on offshore wind energy, could enduringly increase both the amusement value of the trip and the attractiveness of the region. In his review study of a number of papers, [F.] Weickmann concluded that independent of the date and focus of the study, a strong demand for information was seen. He states that 60–75% of respondents indicated a desire for more information regarding offshore wind energy.

In addition, research conducted by Hübner and Pohl shows that 32% of the respondents in 2011 would be interested in an information centre, and 15% of respondents would be interested in boat tours. This would require a close proximity of the wind farm to the coast, since completion of the round trip between harbour and the offshore wind farm site within an acceptable time would be a precondition for making a day trip. Besides their profitability for the region, these edutainment events have benefits concerning education policy, such as education on climate change and the need for alternative energy sources. These educational events could have a multiplier effect, when the information gained is spread to family members, friends or other people.

Additional Benefits

Tourists with a positive attitude towards offshore wind energy perceive an accordance of their own values with the bundle of services offered by the holiday destination as very positive (congruent ideals). Thus the holiday region becomes an expression of their existing values. Among others, dena [Deutsche Energie-Agentur GmbH] proposes that tourism concepts could focus on topical "wind holidays" (e.g. offshore wind energy, kite flying and sailing) or zero emission holidays, which could even be linked to major events related to wind farm construction phases. Moreover, Hilligweg and Kull argue that the promotion of active environmental protection can lead to long-term customer retention. Therefore a well-targeted open information campaign must stress both the aspects related to climate protection and also the importance of offshore wind energy for a region's prosperity.

In addition to the obvious benefits stemming from attractions and values, the offshore wind energy industry spawns regional value creation. New job opportunities result in higher employment rates and thus an increase in purchasing power. Furthermore, both the offshore wind industry itself, and a higher employment rate, lead to higher tax revenues. This in turn may contribute to growing prosperity for the region, attracting more and particularly younger tourists.

Up-to-date public opinion polls on offshore wind energy present an important basis for further discussions. Over the last years, several representative studies have revealed the assumption that tourism will suffer due to offshore wind farms to be more of a subjective fear than a measurable fact. In light of this, offshore wind farms can serve as a tourist attraction, which should be incorporated into regional tourism concepts. This creates an opportunity for the municipality, city, or village to differentiate itself from others in a highly competitive tourism industry and to find a niche market. An increased number of day-trippers and the greater prosperity of a region can influence its development and appeal in a positive manner.

13

The Future of Wind Energy Is Uncertain

Dave Levitan

Dave Levitan is a Philadelphia-based author who writes on the environment, health, and medicine.

Although there is currently only one US offshore wind turbine in operation, many developers are ready to begin projects as soon as the legal hurdles can be cleared. Meanwhile, the Obama administration is attempting to streamline the permitting process to make it easier for developers to begin. Projects also need a financial boost from the government. The entire United States could be powered by wind energy if these hurdles can be overcome, which would allow the country to catch up to other countries when it comes to wind energy development.

In June [2013], after years of offshore wind power projects being thwarted in the United States, the first offshore wind turbine began spinning off the U.S. coast. The turbine was not a multi-megawatt, 400-foot behemoth off of Massachusetts, Rhode Island, New Jersey, or Texas—all places where projects had long been proposed. Rather, the turbine was installed in Castine Harbor, Maine, rising only 60 feet in the air and featuring a 20-kilowatt capacity—enough to power only a few homes.

But it was a turbine—finally. Offshore wind power in the U.S. has struggled mightily to rise from the waves, even as other renewable energy industries have steadily grown. The country now has more than 60,000 megawatts of *onshore* wind, but still just the lone offshore turbine, a pilot project run in part by researchers at the University of Maine. Meanwhile, Europe has left the U.S. far behind, installing its first offshore turbine in 1991 and growing rapidly in the past decade. To date, the countries of the European Union have built 1,939 offshore turbines with 6,040 megawatts of capacity.

U.S. Wind Developers

Is the U.S. offshore wind industry finally about to get off the ground? Offshore wind carries impressive electricity-generating potential, and several projects seem poised to get underway. But energy analysts say the industry still faces daunting hurdles, most notably the higher cost of building offshore wind farms, the expense of connecting them to the onshore grid, and the lack of the comprehensive government incentives and renewable energy targets that have been crucial in fostering the growth of Europe's offshore wind energy sector.

Deepwater Wind hopes to install roughly 200 turbines that could generate more than 1,000 megawatts, enough to power about 400,000 homes.

On the positive side, the infamous Cape Wind project, mired in legal battles for more than a decade, hopes to start construction next year. With plans to construct 130 turbines in the shoals between Nantucket and Cape Cod, Cape Wind has faced enormous legal struggles because of opposition from local residents concerned that the turbines would mar the region's beauty and harm seabird populations. But its legal battles are now largely behind it, and Cape Wind has power-purchase agreements in place. The wind farm's developer, Jim Gordon, says the project will eventually be capable of supplying about 75 percent of the electricity needs of Cape Cod, which has a year-round population of 215,000.

Meanwhile, the Obama administration and the U.S. Department of the Interior have been aggressively moving to streamline permitting processes for offshore wind farms, and this summer completed the first two auctions for large offshore parcels for wind development off the East Coast. Rhode Island-based Deepwater Wind—owned in part by investment firm D.E. Shaw and by First Wind, a Boston-based developer—won the first-ever offshore wind auction held by a division of the Interior Department known as the Bureau of Ocean Energy Management (BOEM). With its winning $3.8 million bid, Deepwater Wind now holds the wind power rights to 165,000 acres off the coasts of Rhode Island and Massachusetts.

"We believe that site is the single best site for offshore wind in the United States," says Deepwater CEO Jeffrey Grybowski, citing the powerful and consistent winds and access to markets in four states—Massachusetts, Rhode Island, Connecticut, and New York. Though the exact number will depend on how much power it can sell to utilities, Deepwater Wind hopes to install roughly 200 turbines that could generate more than 1,000 megawatts, enough to power about 400,000 homes.

A second BOEM auction took place in early September [2013] for a 112,799-acre parcel off the coast of Virginia, this time won by Virginia Electric and Power Company. The planned wind farm could grow as big as 2,000 megawatts. Auctions for sites off of Maryland, New Jersey, and Massachusetts are expected to be held in the next year.

"The more projects we get in the water, the more that will accelerate the development of the industry," says Chris Long, the manager of offshore wind and siting policy at the American Wind Energy Association. "You need to build projects in order to continue innovations, to drive down costs, to achieve scale, and achieve experience. Getting this first round of projects in the water will certainly help to accelerate the development of the industry."

Wind Energy Needs a Boost

At this point, it appears that the first commercial offshore wind installation to begin operating in the U.S. will be Block Island Wind Farm, being developed by Deepwater Wind. Sited about 3 miles from Block Island—itself about 15 miles off the coast of Rhode Island—the wind farm will feature five mammoth turbines, each capable of generating six megawatts. The proposed Block Island installation has the advantage of sitting in state rather than federal waters, easing permitting issues. Grybowski says permitting is all but finished for that project and construction should start next year.

Despite these developments, many analysts are skeptical about the near-term future of offshore wind, especially considering the uncertainty surrounding federal financial support.

A major problem at this point is the high cost of offshore wind.

"Some kind of policy incentive is needed in order to promote offshore wind, since its cost is still far above the market price of electricity," says Bruce Hamilton, director of energy practice at the consulting firm Navigant. Right now, the offshore wind investment tax credit is the only federal incentive, and it is set to expire at the end of 2013 after a one-year extension. It allows developers to take a tax credit on 30 percent of capital expenditures related to a wind project, but construction would have to start this year. Several U.S. senators earlier this year introduced the Incentivizing Offshore Wind Power Act, which would attempt to stabilize the year-to-year policy, but that legislation is likely to die in committee.

"We will [likely] continue to have a stop-start policy at the federal level, since that is what we have experienced for the last couple of decades," Hamilton says.

The uncertainty of federal funding has taken a toll on the proposed Atlantic City Wind Farm off the coast of New Jersey, which would feature five turbines totaling 25 megawatts of capacity. The company behind the project, Fisherman's Energy, was founded by commercial fishermen intent on both developing wind energy and maintaining a strong fishing industry in the region. But the New Jersey Public Utilities Commission is balking at a potential multi-million dollar taxpayer hit if federal funding for the project disappears.

A major problem at this point is the high cost of offshore wind. Because of the difficulty of building wind turbines offshore and connecting them to the power grid, the price of electricity generated offshore along the U.S. East Coast is expected to be more than 15 cents per kilowatt hour, or several times the cost of producing electricity with coal or natural gas, according to a 2012 report by the U.S. National Energy Technology Laboratory. Those costs are expected to fall as more offshore wind farms are built and connected by an offshore grid. Another U.S. report says that a reasonable goal for offshore wind prices would be 10 cents per kilowatt hour by 2020 and 7 cents per kilowatt hour by 2030.

A major project, backed by Google, is planned to link offshore wind farms along the U.S. East Coast to power consumers onshore. The Atlantic Wind Connection is a transmission "backbone" designed to let multiple offshore wind projects essentially plug in to undersea cables as they come online. The first phase, a cable that will stretch the length of the New Jersey coast and be capable of carrying 3,000 megawatts of electricity, is scheduled to begin construction in 2016. The rest of the "backbone" would extend down the coast past Delaware and Maryland, stretching to the coast of Virginia. Along with

Google, the project is funded by such companies as Bregal Energy, Marubeni Corporation, and a Belgian transmission company, Elia.

Long, of the American Wind Energy Association, and others are confident that the initial phase of offshore projects will illustrate to policy makers the attraction of offshore wind power. Onshore wind, after all, is often plagued by siting issues, with nearby residents complaining about the sight and sound of large turbines. Most U.S. offshore projects are now proposed far enough off the coast that they will be essentially invisible—a lesson learned from the "viewshed" controversy surrounding Cape Wind.

The U.S. has no national renewable energy target, but 29 states and Washington, D.C., have adopted their own.

Proponents hope that the start of several offshore projects will encourage more federal and state support and will serve as a reminder that there is a lot of energy just a few miles off the beach.

"The East Coast is the Saudi Arabia of offshore wind, because there is enough energy there to provide the entire U.S. with electricity if it was fully developed," says Matt Huelsenbeck, a marine scientist and offshore wind expert with the non-profit group Oceana. The National Renewable Energy Laboratory, part of the Department of Energy, puts the onshore and offshore U.S. wind energy potential at 4,150 gigawatts, around four times the entire electricity requirements of the United States. The Northeast and mid-Atlantic coasts in particular are windy spots with water depths that make development feasible.

Offshore Wind Has Enormous Potential

The U.S. has no national renewable energy target, but 29 states and Washington, D.C., have adopted their own. Northeastern states like Massachusetts and Rhode Island have been aggressively pursuing renewables, and there is now legislation in New Jersey and Maryland specifically targeting offshore wind development.

Kevin Jones, deputy director of the Institute for Energy and the Environment at the University of Vermont Law School, says he is optimistic about the development of offshore wind, especially in the Northeast, in part because there are so few other options for renewables in the region and the opposition to onshore wind continues to grow.

"If natural gas prices remain low I think the offshore industry is going to need public policy support rather than federal subsidy, but it can happen if the Northeastern states work together to achieve economies of scale," says Jones. That collaboration could include states collectively mandating that utility companies purchase a set amount of electricity from offshore wind farms.

Still, the progress in Europe is a clear reminder of how far the U.S. has to go, a gap that Huelsenbeck attributes to "a failure of our federal government to really back clean energy over the last few decades in a very powerful and consistent way."

The European Union is on target to generate 20 percent of its electricity from renewable sources by 2020, and targets as high as 40 percent are being considered for 2030. In 2014 alone, close to two gigawatts of offshore wind—enough to power more than a million households—are likely to be installed in the EU, with the United Kingdom and Denmark leading the way.

Organizations to Contact

The editors have compiled the following list of organizations concerned with the issues debated in this book. The descriptions are derived from materials provided by the organizations. All have publications or information available for interested readers. The list was compiled on the date of publication of the present volume; the information provided here may change. Be aware that many organizations take several weeks or longer to respond to inquiries, so allow as much time as possible.

American Wind Energy Association (AWEA)
1501 M St. NW, Suite 1000, Washington, DC 20005
(202) 383-2500 • fax: (202) 383-2505
website: www.awea.org

The American Wind Energy Association (AWEA) is the national trade association for the US wind industry. With thousands of wind industry members and wind policy advocates, AWEA promotes wind energy as a clean source of electricity for American consumers. Its mission is to promote wind power growth through advocacy, communication, and education. It educates lawmakers and the public about wind energy, advocates for wind energy policy on Capital Hill and across states, hosts the wind industry's premier annual conference, and conducts research and produces publications on wind energy. Research findings and information about AWEA projects are available on its website.

Bats and Wind Energy Cooperative (BWEC)
website: www.batsandwind.org

The Bats and Wind Energy Cooperative (BWEC) is an alliance of state and federal agencies, private industry, academic institutions, and nongovernmental organizations that cooperates to develop solutions to minimize or, where possible, prevent mortality of bats at wind power turbines. Currently, there are three areas of research BWEC is focusing on: preconstruction monitoring to assess bat activity levels and use at proposed wind turbine sites; postconstruction fatality searches to determine estimates of fatality, compare fatality estimates among facilities, and determine patterns of fatality in relation to weather and habitat variables; and the effectiveness of seasonal low-wind shutdowns and deterring devices on reducing fatality of bats. Information on BWEC's research is available on its website.

Earth Policy Institute (EPI)

1350 Connecticut Ave. NW, Suite 403, Washington, DC   20036
(202) 496-9290 • fax: (202) 496-9325
e-mail: epi@earthpolicy.org
website: www.earth-policy.org

Earth Policy Institute (EPI) works to provide a global plan for moving the world onto an environmentally and economically sustainable path, to provide examples demonstrating how such a plan would work, and to keep the media, policy makers, academics, environmentalists, and other decision makers focused on sustainability. EPI disseminates new information to guide the process of change via its updates, indicators, and books, the most recent of which is *Full Planet, Empty Plates: The New Geopolitics of Food Scarcity*. The organization's website includes numerous publications related to wind energy, including "Cumulative Installed Offshore Wind Power Capacity by Country" and "US Cumulative Installed Wind Power Capacity in Top 10 States."

Energy and Policy Institute

PO Box 15790, Washington, DC   20003
website: www.energyandpolicy.org

The Energy and Policy Institute performs research and analysis on lobbyists, front groups, and politicians working to expand our reliance on fossil fuels and slow the development of a clean energy economy. Through investigative research and strategic communications, the Institute provides Intelligence for the public and policy makers to ensure that we have an honest and transparent debate on energy policy. The group's website contains a special issues section that includes information on wind, solar, and clean energy standards. Information about opponents of clean energy technologies is also available on the website.

Energy Policy Center (EPC) at the Independence Institute

727 E 16th Ave., Denver, CO 80203
(303) 279-6536 • fax: (303) 279-4176
e-mail: info@i2i.org
website: http://energy.i2i.org

As one of the policy centers at the Independence Institute, the goal of the Energy Policy Center (EPC) is to promote a free market in energy production without protections, subsidies, or regulations. EPC believes the best way to ensure that consumers reap the benefits of a healthy energy market is to allow competition, which will result in lower prices and more options. The group's website includes a section devoted to various sources of energy, including wind, with recent news about each of the industries.

Energy Policy Institute (EPI)

1910 University Dr., Boise, ID 83725-1014
(208) 426-5708
e-mail: epi@boisestate.edu
website: http://epi.boisestate.edu

The Energy Policy Institute (EPI) is an integral part of the Center for Advanced Energy Studies, which is a public-private partnership between the Idaho National Laboratory, Boise State University, the University of Idaho, and Idaho State University. EPI provides robust and timely research that meets the challenges of an increasingly carbon-constrained economy, which include the need for energy and environmental security, as well as sustainable economic development, and seeks to inform and educate policy makers and other stakeholders to aid them in making decisions about energy. EPI also hosts the Annual Energy Policy Research Conference. Information on the conference, current research projects, and EPI publications are available on its website.

European Platform Against Windfarms (EPAW)

Drumsallagh, Kingscourt, Co. Cavan
  Republic of Ireland
+33 680 993 808
e-mail: contact@epaw.org
website: www.epaw.org

The European Platform Against Windfarms (EPAW) is based in Ireland and has 675 member organizations from twenty-four countries. The aim of EPAW is to defend the interests of its members that are either opposing one or more wind farm proposals; questioning the effectiveness of wind farms as a tool for solving the problems of humanity and the planet; or defending the flora, fauna, and landscapes from damage caused by wind farms, directly or through environmental degradation such as erosion, water contamination, and bush fires; or generally fighting against the damaging effects of wind farms on tourism, the economy, people's quality of life, the value of their properties, and, increasingly, their health; or a combination of the above. The organization's website contains links to wind energy news from around the world.

European Wind Energy Association (EWEA)

website: www.ewea.org

It is the objective of the European Wind Energy Association (EWEA) to facilitate national and international policies and initiatives that strengthen the development of European and global wind energy markets, infrastructure, and technology in order to achieve a more sustainable and cleaner energy future. To achieve this, EWEA acts as a single European voice to promote, through the joint efforts of its members, the best interest of the wind energy sector. EWEA's website includes copies of reports and position papers as well as a blog, press releases, and video clips.

National Wind Watch (NWW)

63 West Hill Rd., Hawley, MA   01339
e-mail: query@wind-watch.org
website: www.wind-watch.org

National Wind Watch (NWW) is a coalition of groups and individuals working to preserve rural and wild places from industrial wind energy development. Through its website, NWW promotes awareness and documents the negative impacts of industrial-scale wind turbines on the environment, economy, and quality of life of those who live in surrounding areas. It also aims to be a resource of information and assistance for individuals and local groups seeking information about industrial wind power. The NWW website includes news items, fact sheets, and research links.

Natural Resources Defense Council (NRDC)

40 West 20th St., New York, NY   10011
(212) 727-2700 • fax: (212) 727-1773
e-mail: nrdcinfo@nrdc.org
website: www.nrdc.org

The Natural Resources Defense Council (NRDC) is an environmental action group focused on curbing global warming, creating clean energy, reviving the world's oceans, prevention pollution, ensuring safe and sufficient water, and fostering sustainable communities. The NRDC website includes "Renewable Energy for America," a guide on US energy with maps, technology basics, and state profiles.

350.org

20 Jay St., Suite 1010, Brooklyn, NY   11201
(518) 635-0350
e-mail: team@350.org
website: http://350.org

The organization 350.org drew its name from scientist recommendations that in order to preserve a livable planet the amount of carbon dioxide in the atmosphere must be reduced from its current level of 400 parts per million to below 350 parts per million. The organization believes that a global grassroots movement can hold our leaders accountable to the realities of science and the principles of justice. It uses distributed, grassroots organizing to run adaptive, locally driven campaigns across the globe. The organization's website includes information on current projects and campaigns on alternative energy, including wind and solar power.

US Department of Energy, Office of Energy Efficiency and Renewable Energy (EERE)

1000 Independence Ave. SW, Washington, DC 20585
(877) 337-3463
website: www.energy.gov

The mission of the US Department of Energy is to ensure America's security and prosperity by addressing its energy, environmental, and nuclear challenges through transformative science and technology solutions. Within the US Department of Energy, the Office of Energy Efficiency and Renewable Energy (EERE) leads efforts to build a strong, clean energy economy, create a strategy that is aimed at reducing our reliance on foreign oil, save families and businesses money, create middle-class jobs, and reduce pollution. The agency's website hosts a large section devoted to wind energy and includes information on wind energy basics, wind turbine manufacturing, wind resource maps and data, offshore wind technology, and environment and siting of wind projects.

US Environmental Protection Agency (EPA)

1200 Pennsylvania Ave. NW, Washington, DC 20460
(202) 272-0167
website: www.epa.gov

The US Environmental Protection Agency (EPA) was established to consolidate in one agency a variety of federal research, monitoring, standard-setting, and enforcement activities to ensure environmental protection. Since its inception, EPA has been working for a cleaner, healthier environment for the American people. EPA's purpose is to ensure that all Americans are protected from significant risks to human health and the environment where they live, learn, and work. To accomplish this mission, the EPA develops and enforces regulations, gives grants, studies environmental issues, forms sponsor partnerships, teaches people about the environment, and publishes related information via its website.

US Offshore Wind Collaborative (USOWC)

1 Broadway, 14th Floor, Cambridge, MA   02142
(617) 401-3145
website: http://usoffshorewind.org

The US Offshore Wind Collaborative (USOWC) works to help coastal and Great Lakes states make offshore wind energy available. Initiatives include the Offshore Supply Chain Working Group, which supports and advances regional development; and the Offshore WindHub, which is a web-based information clearinghouse with information from key state and federal agencies concerning Atlantic Coast offshore wind energy development. The group's website also includes a blog and links to other organizations supporting offshore wind technologies and development.

Wind Energy Foundation (WEF)

1501 M St. NW, Suite 900, Washington, DC   20005
(202) 383-2552
e-mail: info@windenergyfoundation.org
website: www.windenergyfoundation.org

The Wind Energy Foundation (WEF) is a nonprofit organization dedicated to raising public awareness of wind as a clean, domestic energy source through communication, research, and education. Information on the campaigns and programs, grants and scholarships, and research of WEF is available on its website. The website also contains educational materials for students from kindergarten through college.

Bibliography

Books

Godfrey Boyle   *Renewable Energy: Power for a Sustainable Future.* New York: Oxford University Press, 2012.

Lester R. Brown   *Plan B4.0: Mobilizing to Save Civilization.* New York: W.W. Norton, 2009.

Robert Bryce   *Power Hungry.* New York: PublicAffairs, 2011.

Robert Bryce   *Smaller Faster Lighter Denser Cheaper.* New York: PublicAffairs, 2014.

Dan Chiras   *The Homeowner's Guide to Renewable Energy: Achieving Energy Independence Through Solar, Wind, Biomass, and Hydropower.* Gabriola Island, British Columbia, Canada: New Society Publishers, 2011.

Dan Chiras   *Wind Power Basics: A Green Energy Guide.* Gabriola Island, British Columbia, Canada: New Society Publishers, 2013.

Allan Drummond   *Energy Island: How One Community Harnessed the Wind and Changed Their World.* New York: Farrar, Straus and Giroux, 2011.

Rody Johnson

Chasing the Wind: Inside the Alternative Energy Battle. Knoxville: University of Tennessee Press, 2014.

David J.C. MacKay

Sustainable Energy—Without the Hot Air. Cambridge, UK: UIT Cambridge, 2009.

Kevin Shea and Brian Clark Howard

Build Your Own Small Wind Power System. New York: McGraw-Hill, 2011.

Jeremy Shere

Renewable: The World-Changing Power of Alternative Energy. New York: St. Martin's Press, 2013.

Philip Warburg

Harvest the Wind: America's Journey to Jobs, Energy Independence, and Climate Stability. Boston: Beacon Press, 2012.

Roland Wengenmayr

Renewable Energy: Sustainable Energy Concepts for the Energy Change. Hoboken, NJ: Wiley, 2012.

Ozzie Zehner

Green Illusions: The Dirty Secrets of Clean Energy and the Future of Environmentalism. Lincoln: University of Nebraska Press, 2012.

Periodicals and Internet Sources

Carol Atkinson-Palombo and Ben Hoen

"Relationship Between Wind Turbines and Residential Property Values in Massachusetts," Electricity Markets and Policy Group, 2014. http://emp.lbl.gov.

Ben Bryant — "National Trust Director-General: Wind Turbines are Beautiful," *The Telegraph*, February 24, 2013.

Robert Bryce — "Dreaming the Impossible Green Dream," *Wall Street Journal*, June 11, 2014. http://online.wsj.com.

Diane Cardwell — "Tax Credit in Doubt; Wind Power Industry Is Withering," *New York Times*, September 20, 2012.

Damian Carrington — "Why There's Only One Honest Objection to Wind Farms," *The Guardian*, June 21, 2012.

Matt A.V. Chaban — "Turbines Popping Up on New York Roofs, Along with Questions of Efficiency," *New York Times*, May 26, 2014.

Stephen Gibbons — "Gone with the Wind: Valuing the Visual Impacts of Wind Turbines through House Prices," Spatial Economics Research Center, April 2014. www.spatialeconomics.ac.uk.

Simon Gourlay — "Wind Farms Are Not Only Beautiful, They're Absolutely Necessary," *The Guardian*, August 11, 2008.

Joshua S. Hill — "Wind Farms Might Affect House Prices After All," CleanTechnica, 2014. http://cleantechnica.com.

Independent   "The Conservatives Are Deciding
                          Wind Farm Applications on the Basis
                          of their Appearance. This is
                          Misguided," June 11, 2014.

Steve LeBlanc   "More Ocean off Massachusetts
                          Open for Wind Energy," ABCNews,
                          June 17, 2014. http://abcnews.go.com.

Jay Lehr   "Wind Turbines: American's Vast,
                          Ugly Sculpture Garden," *Heartlander
                          Magazine*, July 16, 2013.
                          http://news.heartland.org.

Alexis C.   "When Lightning Strikes a Huge
Madrigal   Wind Turbine," *The Atlantic*, June 15,
                          2014.

Tess McRae   "The Windy City Is Actually in
                          Queens," *Queens Chronicle*, June 12,
                          2014. www.qchron.com.

Oliver Milman   "Joe Hockey Tilts at Wind Turbines,"
                          The Guardian, May 1, 2014.

Jim Platts   "Offshore Wind Is Too Expensive,"
                          The Ecologist, December 2013.
                          www.theecologist.org.

John Rogers   "The Effect of Wind Turbines on
                          Property Values: A New Study in
                          Massachusetts Provides Some
                          Answers," Union of Concerned
                          Scientists, January 22, 2014.
                          http://blog.ucsusa.org.

Stephen Rowland   "'Avian Holocaust': Protecting Wind
                          Farms Is Killing Birds," *Columbia
                          Daily Herald*, June 11, 2014.

Matthew L. Wald   "An Argument Over Wind," *New York Times*, September 14, 2012. http://green.blogs.nytimes.com.

Index

$29.96   4/22/15

LONGWOOD PUBLIC LIBRARY
800 Middle Country Road
Middle Island, NY 11953
(631) 924-6400
longwoodlibrary.org

LIBRARY HOURS

Monday-Friday	9:30 a.m. - 9:00 p.m.
Saturday	9:30 a.m. - 5:00 p.m.
Sunday (Sept-June)	1:00 p.m. - 5:00 p.m.